HERDSMEN AND HERMITS

By the same Author

MERLIN'S ISLAND

UPERNIVIK FJORD, WEST GREENLAND IN 1937 A.D.

This picture might just as well represent a view taken from the north end of Kerrera and looking up towards Fort William about ten thousand years ago.

HERDSMEN & HERMITS

Celtic Seafarers in the Northern Seas

T. C. LETHBRIDGE

M.A., F.S.A.

Honorary Keeper of Anglo-Saxon Antiquities,
University Museum of Archaeology and of Ethnology, Cambridge

Foreword by

T. D. KENDRICK

F.B.A., F.S.A.

Director and Principal Librarian of the British Museum

BOWES & BOWES · CAMBRIDGE

First published in 1950 by
Bowes and Bowes Publishers Limited, Cambridge

Printed by Balding and Mansell Ltd, Park Works, Wisbech

FOREWORD

by

T. D. KENDRICK, F.B.A., F.S.A.

Director and Principal Librarian of the British Museum

TOM LETHBRIDGE asked me to write an introduction to this book in about three lines of a long letter about a variety of quite different subjects. I asked him why he wanted me to perform such an unnecessary task, and he replied that he had forgotten his reason, if any, for making the request, but he hoped that I would help him to trace an enshrined arm of St Etheldreda that had been removed from Ely Cathedral, hidden in Sussex, discovered on the Duke of Norfolk's property, and was now believed to be preserved in a midland nunnery. I applied again for some justification of my appearance in this foreword and was sent in answer an exciting new theory about the origin of the Mildenhall Treasure. I feel, therefore, that I can say what I like, and what I have to say is, obviously, that this most interesting book by an already established writer does not need any introduction at all. His readers will realize at once that it is a fine thing, and to many of them its author is well known as an important archaeologist with a vigorously original mind. If you turn to page 71 and begin five lines from the bottom, 'What does it matter if the dates are wrong'. . . ; and continue to the end of this paragraph on page 72, you will have some measure of the power and unforced eloquence of this remarkable author who has told us that he cannot spell and could never learn grammar. Tom Lethbridge combines a well-balanced and appreciative understanding of the life of our distant forerunners with a determined belief that these people were no better than they ought to have been. Nevertheless he likes them a lot when they are fighting and stealing, and he does not mind them being lousy; and it is plain that he likes them best of all when they are bravely at sea in what seem to us to be rather ridiculous little boats. It is here that he reveals a wonderful practical knowledge of their problems, and it is here that his opinions, on such subjects, for instance, as the early voyages in northern waters, become almost aggressively memorable, even when one has decided not to believe in them. 'This pretty picture may be absolutely incorrect,' he remarks cheerfully when talking of the broch people (page 50), and this characteristic comment illustrates another aspect of his work, for he would not in the least mind anyone saying that other things in the book may also be absolutely incorrect. What he offers us is a personal interpretation that he knows must bring us closer to the peoples he is studying, and will prove in itself a valuable essay in method. It is enough for the author that his pretty picture of the herdsmen and hermits of north-western Europe is as helpful a vision as he can now give us, and I think he may be fully assured that many will hereafter benefit from this richly detailed sketch. The dreadful glimpse of the trussed and kippered bodies of Beaker Men slung at the side of horses for conveyance to distant barrows where they are destined to become our 'crouched burials', is, to give just one example, the kind of vision that, whether it be right or wrong, can hardly fail to turn us all into interested friends of the Early Bronze Age.

ACKNOWLEDGEMENTS

Once, during the war, I found it necessary to speak in sorrow to a village headman. 'This platoon is in a disgraceful state,' I said. 'The turn-out is appalling; the arms are dirty, and the men are untrained. I don't think you have the slightest idea how many men you have on your books, what weapons have been issued, or how much ammunition you hold'. He looked at me sadly for a moment and then replied brightly 'I admit it all, sir.' Well, I admit all Tom Kendrick said in the first paragraph of the undeservedly flattering foreword he has so kindly written for me. I have, however, remembered the reason why I asked him to write it. It was a clever idea I had of trying to find out what he really thought of the thing. The letters which pass between us are so full of cynical banter and jocular untruth that, like the two Canadian Mounties I met at Craig Harbour, it is impossible for the one to believe what the other says without some formal guarantee.

The situation at Craig Harbour was like this. If one policeman came in and said 'I saw a mighty big bear down on the shore,' the other took not the slightest notice. If, however, the first man said, 'I saw a mighty big bear down on the shore. Cross me heart and spit for death,' the second man instantly snatched up his rifle and ran to the door. The foreword in this book takes the place of the mounties' 'Cross me heart and spit for death.' I am very grateful to him for writing it and at the same time I feel a bit embarrassed.

My wife has had again the sorry task of deciphering my untidy manuscript and typing it out in the garden surrounded by 'myriads of loathsome stinging creatures'.

Miss Clare Fell and Mr C. F. Tebbutt have encouraged me by reading the typescript and giving me many useful suggestions.

B

Finally, I should like to thank the Publishers. Without the encouragement of Mr Denis Payne I should not have bothered to write the book and I suspect also that he has unobtrusively tidied up some of my more uncouth phrases.

T. C. LETHBRIDGE

CONTENTS

TEXT ILLUSTRATIONS

INTRODUCTION

THIS IS NOT a text book of Scottish, Icelandic or Eskimo archaeology. Anyone who reads it can see that the writing of such a work today is not only impossible, it is almost an impertinence. I am writing for two reasons. One is entirely selfish; to amuse myself by gathering together all the ideas on this subject that have been accumulating in my head since I first went to the North. These ideas are not only archaeological; they include suggestions about historical, anthropological, geographical and even geological problems, the existence of which in some cases has not even been realized. The second reason is of a more kindly nature. It seems to me that very many people would be interested to learn more about the early peoples of Scotland, particularly the west of Scotland, and also of the countries to the north of it; how and when their settlements were formed and how the people lived.

It will be seen that we do not know very much, but what we do know makes us only the keener to learn more. I feel that few people have any idea that there was an ancient, though often interrupted, connexion between Scotland, Iceland and even Greenland. It is of course understood that the relationship between Scotland and Ireland has always been close, but it may not be realized how it can be proved to have existed age after age by archaeological discoveries. The whole book is lamentably full of question marks, and doubtless errors, not only of grammar, which I never succeeded in learning at school, but also of interpretation. I am not ashamed of the second type, for archaeology is like a detective story and we all follow up the wrong clues at times.

Had that old warrior, the late Professor Sir William Ridgeway, been alive, I hope he would not have described my efforts as 'mere maundering', as he did the learned work of one of his colleagues. I do not think, however, that he would. He was too fond of 'the old devils', as he affectionately described the ancient heroes of Britain and Ireland, to disapprove of anything that could add to their fame. Although I deal more with seafaring monks and pirates than with horsemen and chariots, the same courage and hardihood which inspired their brothers to throw the javelin or swing the sword sent them far over the seas in flimsy boats. I sometimes grin when I remember the remark he made to me about the effigies of knights in churches. People piously explain that they are sheathing their swords with their duty done. 'The old devils', said Ridgeway. 'They were drawing them'. He cannot be considered quite free from blame himself, for he left the most fascinating essay on the Heroic Age of Ireland to be buried in a book on *The Early Age of Greece*, where few people ever find it.

There are plenty of old devils still in the world, who would rather be making a long passage in a small boat than bawling into a telephone at an office desk. I hope this falls into the hands of one or two of them and gives them some pleasure. I think, however, I must belong to the last generation that can ever hope to see new lands for the first time from the deck of a ship. When we were on a passage from Cape Wrath to Cape Farewell in 1937, and lying hove-to in a North Atlantic blow, the first Sunderland flying-boat passed serenely to the south of us on her way to America. I thought at the time that we were probably on about the last voyage of discovery in the North, and so we were. Now you can fly over any country and 'discover' it by air photography.

The old devils have little chance in the world today, but the spirit is still there and cannot be crushed. When everyone has been measured up, and all the statisticians know exactly how many calories it takes to feed the average man, exactly how he will react to any given stimulus, exactly how much it will cost to clothe and feed him exactly like all his fellows, the old devils will emerge again and show them that they have forgotten something in their calculations. For no man is exactly like his fellows, or wishes to be so. One single man with guts and ginger will always be of more value than ten thousand without it. Why was it that Patrick could convert the heathen Irish, and Columba the Picts? It was just because they were not like other men, but had fire in their blood. Very likely they were spurred on by pains in the stomach, rotten teeth, or some such thing; King Alfred and St. Paul appear to have been afflicted in this way. They were all old devils in the service of God.

Throughout this book I have tried to cut down the number of technical terms to the barest limit. This is not because I am unacquainted with their use, but because I know well that whenever I see a book full of terms which I have to look up in a Greek or Latin Dictionary, I am always tempted to fling it in the fire. I could make up plenty of technical terms myself if need be. They are, however, as often as not, a sign of the inability of their author to express himself in simple words. Anthropologists and psychologists coin more technical jargon than any other breed of scientist, but archaeologists are pretty bad. This mumbo-jumbo is greatly to be deplored, for it gives all their work a bogus appearance. I have listened to a heated interchange of words between two anthropologists about the meaning of the term 'skeuomorph.' They became quite angry, because neither could understand what the other meant by this. Nobody knew at the end.

Although this book is short, and I hope relatively simple, it is the result of a great deal of study. I have read every book I can lay hands on that appears to have any bearing on the subjects briefly discussed in it. Had I wished it could have been made twice the size, with references to some scores of books and probably hundreds of papers and monographs. It is not intended, however, as a handy book of reference to the archaeology of the North, but rather as a kind of summary of what we appear to know and what remains to be learnt. The credit side is pretty weak.

Many references and footnotes in a book, although they may give it the appearance of wide learning, are a perfect pest to the reader, and continually break his train of thought. This time I will leave them almost all out. I know that nobody will regret their absence.

One very kindly critic of a former book of mine accused me of having a nostalgia for the past. This is not so at all. I look on the present age as every bit as exciting and romantic as any age that preceded it. I can, however, appreciate the sadness which comes at the end of one age and the rawness at the beginning of the next. I can see just as much beauty in the glistening hull of a great air-liner as in that of a four-masted barque. There is no traveller or explorer that I have ever met, who has not spent much of his time on his journeys in arguing with his companions what they will have to eat at their first meal when they get home. The first hot bath is looked forward to with as much pleased anticipation as that with which a saint prepared himself for Heaven. I may take a great delight in the study of the past, but I also enjoy what are left of the comforts of the present day.

Few people can really appreciate the life of long ago, unless they have lived for a time in conditions which resemble it. I can hear my aunts exclaiming, when they read of the lice in the shirts of Dicuil's monks: 'Oh, poor men, how terrible it must have been for them!' It was nothing of the kind: they were always lousy. Everybody was after the fall of Rome, until Beau Brummell taught the Englishmen to 'wash their strength away'. Scabies, ringworm and toothache were seldom absent. The past, though it may seem romantic now, was full of dirt, boredom, discomfort and disease, which is hard to understand today. Think of the smell and filth of a medieval castle, with the garderobe shoots opening on to the moat. The knights and ladies seldom washed; they had lice in their heads; they could hardly read or write. There was little to do but work, hunt, make love, or prepare for war. Equally tedious was the existence of a chieftain in Iceland. His life was limited to his farming and to the management of his estate, with occasional work at his forge or a sea expedition to catch his winter cod; there was no variety in it at all, except the annual journey to the Thing where he could meet his friends and relations. He could not read or write. In the long winter evenings, especially when there was plenty of beer, fancied grievances, such as the straying of a neighbour's sheep, grew to terrific proportions. The women egged the men on and then somebody was killed.

It is easy to see why men took to piracy. It is easy to see too why men went out in search of solitude to meditate. The voyage to the far north was a blissful relief. In fine weather the curragh's motion over the long swells would soothe any jangled nerves. In bad weather it was not much worse than the hard work in the monastery fields and much more exciting. If you were drowned, you went to heaven and saw all the Blessed Saints. If you came back in safety, you were something of a hero.

Then again, people speak with horror of the discomforts of the settlers' life in Greenland. Greenland is an enormous country. In summer you never need anything warmer than a tweed coat down where the Norsemen used to live. It was cold in winter no doubt, but the fug inside the houses would soon warm you up. Why, the Eskimos, like the ancient Irish, always invited a visitor to take all his clothes off when coming inside their huts.

There was nothing heroic done by men in the past, which has not been done by civilized men in the present century. Look at the marvellous voyages made in ships' life-boats. Shackleton's boat voyage to South Georgia beats anything that any Viking ever did. I doubt too whether you could have made a Viking army stay in London while it was being bombed, and turn out night after night to deal with incendiaries. There is no question of men not being so courageous as they were in days of old. They are every bit as brave, steadfast and loyal, but they are more thoughtful, too, and perform acts of courage which in old time could only have been done under the influence of drink, stupidity or wild rage. Now they do them because they know by reasoning that they must and they are only supported by a cup of tea. When one is tempted to think that it was incredibly brave of monks to sail to Iceland in a skin boat, it is easy to see the matter in its proper perspective by remembering our war-time convoys passing round the north of Norway between the pack-ice and the German bombers, or even the trawler men in the arctic winter working their nets off Bear Island from ice-covered decks. There may have been heroes and giants in the old days, but there are just as many among us now.

> The heroes of antiquity ne'er saw the cannon ball;
> Nor felt the force of powder to scatter foes withal.

I may seem to be writing rather disparagingly about all this. There is, however, another side to the picture. Can anyone imagine a modern artist sitting down in a tiny, dark hut and probably spending his whole working life in the illumination of the Book of Kells or Lindisfarne? How on earth did he work out his beautiful and complicated patterns, with no rough paper to scribble on? It seems that he probably drew them first with a stick on a flattened heap of sand or fine ashes. Sometimes he scratched them on pieces of dry bone. When he had got them right, he spent weeks and weeks in a very bad light getting them on to vellum. There is no need to give much honour to modern painters who slash off some rubbish on a canvas in a few hours and call it 'art'. I had a friend, who with two others, rushed through a series of 'modern' paintings as a joke. They hired a room and held an exhibition. All the critics and the intelligentsia were taken in and spoke highly of it. Nobody can do that with Celtic art. So let us remember kindly the nameless men who ruined their eyesight in creating beautiful books and metalwork in the seventh or eighth centuries, even if most of their labour was torn up by pirates to provide knick-knacks for Norwegian peasant women.

Finally, I am writing the book with a background of personal experience, and am not like Strabo, who criticized

Pytheas from the security of his library. I have crossed all the seas mentioned in it in ships of under a hundred tons burden, and have wandered on the shores of all the lands, except Wineland the Good. Once, long ago, I had the good luck to take part in the first ascent of the old, ice-covered volcano of Berenberg in Jan Mayen. When we reached the crater rim, which formed the summit, we could see nothing but a knife-edge of snow; everything else was fog. Presently the clouds began to shift and we could look down on to a new land spread below us and seen through a gap in the mountain basin. Glaciers, hills, valleys and the Arctic Ocean suddenly appeared. Archaeology is like that. At first all is fog; then the sun breaks through and you begin to see new peoples and new lands. It is quite as exciting as climbing mountains.

CHAPTER ONE

THE EARLIEST MEN OF THE ISLANDS

SOME THREE HUNDRED YEARS before Julius Cæsar first looked out over the Channel at the shore of Britain, Pytheas, a scientific geographer of Massilia in Southern Gaul, set out to test his ideas of the measurement of the earth and to gain some first-hand knowledge of the northern parts of Europe. He was probably one of the greatest adventurers the world has known, but the facts with which he returned after years of travel did not conform to the ideas of the sedentary geographers. Pytheas' published results appear to have been lost beyond recall, but, by a pleasing irony, many scraps of information which he collected, probably at great risk to himself, have been preserved in the violently abusive writings of his critics. He went far beyond the limits ascribed by traditional learning to the habitable earth. He found people living beyond these limits. Therefore he must have been a phenomenal liar. A Victorian explorer saw gorillas building nests in trees and duly reported this fact to the Royal Geographical Society, only to meet with similar abuse. The explorer, however, had the chance, so the story goes, to spit in his detractor's face in a London street; Pytheas never had the opportunity of meeting Strabo, Polybius and the rest. We now know that much of what Pytheas said was true. Geographical and archaeological study have refuted the critics.

The surviving scraps of information gathered in Pytheas' travels have been carefully collected, weighed and considered by many students. They are of great interest to us, for they provide the first written account of Britain before the days of Cæsar. Many things can be checked. Kantion is still Kent; Orcas still survives in the name of the Orkneys. The underground cellars for the storage of grain have been excavated in many Iron Age camps. The chiefs used chariots and their graves have been found in Yorkshire. The people of Belerion, he said, which was then the name of Cornwall, were more civilized than the rest in the Prettanic Isles. They mined tin with great skill, hammered it into pieces like dice and carried it in carts at low tide to Ictis, which was six days' sail in skin boats from somewhere no longer known. Some think that the six days' sail was from the mouth of the Loire round Uxisame, which is still Ushant. In any case, we know that the Cornishmen had been mining tin for hundreds of years before Pytheas reported it.

One of the most interesting questions raised by Pytheas' voyage, however, is the problem of Thule. Thule was at the end of the habitable world, but it was habitable. It is uncertain whether Pytheas went there himself, but it seems most probable that he did. Pytheas was a geographer, and his main quest was the measurement of the sun's declination at various points on the longest day of the year. The great point about Thule was that it had a day when the sun never set at all. Thule was therefore on the Arctic Circle. It was six days' sail from Britain. All depends on the length of a day's sail and from whence you start. In the days of Bede in the eighth century A.D., Britain was still six days' sail from Thule. The Icelanders, in the days of the Norse Settlement, had little doubt that Thule was Iceland, as is stated in the prologue to the *Landnamabok*. A day's sail is therefore a measure of distance, possibly based on an average of many passages. It is probably about ninety miles, but may be more or may be less. One day's sailing northward of Thule something was reported by Pytheas, which was worse than any gorilla's nest. He had seen it from a distance. This was the frozen, or curdled, sea. It was neither land, nor sea, nor air, but a kind of mixture of all three. It was like a 'sea lung', which probably means a 'Portuguese Man-of-War' or nautilus, in which everything floats. It was impossible for men or ships to get through it. This is no doubt a garbled account of what Pytheas really described, but it is a description which anyone, who has seen the edge of the Polar pack ice in a fog, will recognize at once. The mass of tiny fragments of brash ice and the little floes all rising and falling in the swell, half seen in the grey blanket of fog, might well be described as a sea lung. They hiss and fret with the movement of the sea as if they were breathing. At the right time of year, millions of little auks sit about on the bits of ice making a tiny peeping noise to their babies. It is like nothing else in the world. I can see it now, if I shut my eyes, and no doubt Pytheas could too, years after he returned to sunny Massilia. Stefansson, the explorer, saw the resemblance, but it would mean nothing to someone sitting in a library in Italy. The curdled sea, however, had come to stay in the minds of men. When, more than three hundred years later, Agricola's fleet passed through Fair Isle Channel northward of the Orkneys, the seamen believed they could see Thule, and imagined that they saw the curdled sea.

There are some who think that Pytheas never went near Iceland, and look for Thule on the coast of Norway; but Pytheas saw the curdled sea and described the midnight sun. He could have seen the midnight sun without difficulty in Norway, but the curdled sea would have been hundreds of miles away. Even if Pytheas never went to Iceland himself, somebody was going there. Here is a problem of the greatest interest. Who was sailing to Iceland, and why did they sail so far over the grey northern waters? How long had they been going and did they go still further? Before the days of Pytheas there had been great navigators in Western Europe. The men who brought the idea of Megalithic monuments round by sea from Spain to France, to England and Ireland, also reached the Hebrides and Orkneys. Did they pass on by way of the Faeroes to Iceland? There seems little doubt that they could have done so. Long years of observation of the migrations of birds would have told them there was land up in the north, where birds could find food in the summer; if birds could go, so could they. No one has yet found a trace of them.

The Shetlands were peopled from the Bronze Age onwards. Shetlanders could have gone north. No one has found a trace of them either, not even in the Faeroes.

Someone, however, in the days of Pytheas, knew all about Thule, the pack ice and the midnight sun. He did not invent these things. They are as much real facts as the store pits for grain and the tin trade. The difficulty is that, before the days of Pytheas, those who could read and write had no contact with the north to any appreciable extent. The rich Bronze Age civilizations of Britain, Ireland or Denmark were beyond the knowledge of the Mediterranean peoples. No one in the south had the slightest idea what was happening to the north of them. If merchants obtained luxuries, like amber or furs, from the north, they were not ready to talk much about how they managed the trade, for talk might encourage competition. Stories of the freezing of the Baltic in winter encouraged southern geographers to believe that the habitable world ended far south of where in fact it did.

It lies therefore in the hands of archaeologists to dig out the history of the Northern Lands, which lay beyond the reach of any southern historian. The visitors to Thule, before the voyage of Pytheas, were probably seeking things of value to chieftains in Britain. These may have been polar-bear and blue-fox skins, with the possible addition of walrus hides and ivory.

To carry the story any further, it is now necessary to turn to the picture of early Britain which is gradually being drawn for us by the efforts of many students, whose examination of ancient documents, old earthworks and dwelling-sites increases our knowledge day by day. The work of botanists and geologists, who are piecing together the story of the changes in climate which have taken place since the Great Ice Age, must also have its part in the making of this picture.

If, on a summer day towards the end of the Ice Age, a man could have climbed a hill in Arran, Mull or Skye, and looked towards the mainland of Scotland, he would have seen a picture almost exactly like a view in Greenland today. The sea lochs would be filled with floating icebergs of various shapes and sizes. Some, as big as cathedrals and as fantastically pinnacled, would be stranded on the shallows; others of small size would be drifting clear and floating majestically out to sea. Inland all but a few rocks at the tops of the hills would be covered by an immense glittering mass of ice, which, as it neared the coast, would be intersected by thousands of great crevasses. Tongues from this great ice sheet would be creeping down what are now the glens, and pushing out into the lochs as great floating cliffs. The watcher on the hill would hear frequent roars and growls as the sea, moving beneath these cliffs, detached great lumps, which floated away as bergs. Islands, like Bute or Kerrera, would not stand as high as they do today, for the great weight of the central ice sheet, thousands of feet thick and hundreds of miles in length, was enough to depress the crust of the earth beneath it. Looking down the slopes to the land beneath him, the man would see bare, rocky ground. Nothing grew here as it grows now. Clumps of saxifrage, tufts of dryas, Iceland poppies or dwarf willows, with occasional patches of rough grass, would be the limit of vegetation. Rocks would stand out nakedly, for no blanket of peat or soil had yet formed to clothe their sides. So far as we know, no man ever saw this sight in Scotland.[1]

Perhaps eight thousand years ago, the ice had left Scotland. Freed from its enormous weight, the land began to rise and the cliffs of the former sea stand back from it now, with the shallows at their feet spread out before them. These are the raised beaches so familiar in western Scotland. They show signs of much fiercer sea action than anything comparable today. All round the Firth of Lorne, for instance, caves are found in the cliffs of the beach, which stands about twenty-five feet above the modern sea level. If an allowance is made for the sinking of the land by this twenty-five feet, it is clear that the dimensions of the Firth would not be greatly increased. But caves were cut in places where the sea could have only had a very few miles carry in which to raise waves fierce enough to cut deeply into the cliffs. No comparable caves appear to be in process of formation today. Whether the throwing of blocks of ice at the cliffs would have had any appreciable effect, I cannot say, but I have not observed the results of any such pounding in Greenland. On the whole, it appears probable that the sea, which formed the twenty-five foot-raised beach, achieved its rock-cutting because the level remained unchanged for a very long period. In this case, the present sea level has not been in existence for anything like so long a time. This is perhaps confirmed by the undoubted disappearance in historic times of much of the western coast of the Hebrides beneath the waves.

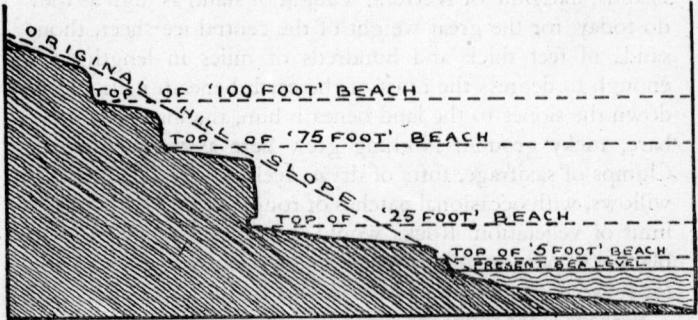

HIGHLY SIMPLIFIED SECTION OF THE RAISED BEACHES AROUND THE FIRTH OF LORNE

The 100 foot and 75 foot beaches are earlier than the last glaciation. There are probably other beaches also.

The twenty-five-foot raised beach is important, because on it have been found the dwelling sites of the earliest known people in western Scotland. They have been compared with the Azilian people of France, who are thought to have lived in French caves not long after the end of the glacial period in Europe. In caves in Oban and on the storm beach of the twenty-five-foot raised beach in Oransay, there have been found extensive remains of a people using stone tools and bone harpoons. They ate enormous quantities of shell-fish, speared grey mullet in the shallows, and caught great auks for food. They must have been boatmen, for otherwise their appearance in islands far out from the land is impossible. The extreme antiquity of these people is, however, doubtful. In the Oban caves their remains have been found on sand on the cave floor, which is thought to have been deposited by the twenty-five-foot beach sea. On Oransay their dwelling sites were on top of the storm beach of this sea. It was thought that little time could have elapsed since this sea receded. I have myself, however, explored a small cave on the twenty-five-foot

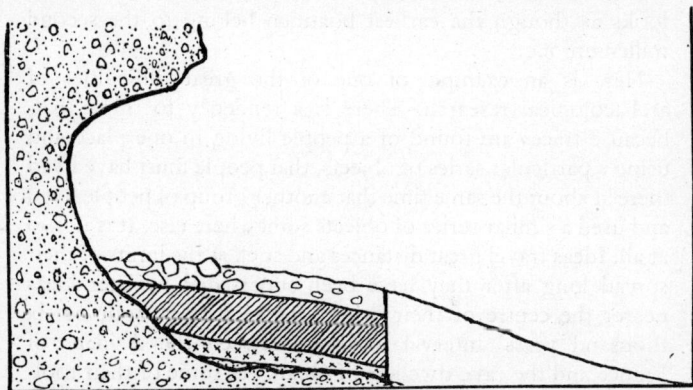

| [○°] =Rock | [○°] =Modern Occupation | ▨ =Sterile Layer | [ˣ ˣ ˣ] =Ancient Occupation |

Greatest thickness of deposits is 3 feet.

SECTION OF ROCK-SHELTER ON TOP OF THE '25 FOOT' RAISED BEACH AT ARDANTRIVE, KERRERA, ARGYLL

The ancient occupation layer yielded limpet-hammers, fragments of 'Neolithic' pottery, a broken leaf-shaped flint arrow-head and a pigmy flint scraper similar to those found on 'Beaker' sites. The term 'limpet-hammer' is used advisedly for, in spite of the contrary opinion of some experts, they are still known by the Gaelic equivalent of that name in the West of Scotland. The limpet-hammer is a smooth beach-pebble often some 7 inches long with two pronounced bevels worn at one end by knocking limpets off the rocks. Anyone can produce similar bevels by experiment.

raised beach on Kerrera. This faced the Oban caves at the distance of about a mile. On the very floor of this little cave, and lying either on the bare rock, or on patches of sand, were traces of early occupation. The cave was damp and almost all trace of bones and shells had disappeared, but flint and stone implements were comparatively numerous. These included part of a leaf-shaped flint arrowhead and scrapers of flint, but there were also fragments of pottery. There can be little doubt that these objects are not older than about 2000 B.C. They probably belong to a period later than that, when the Early Bronze Age was in full swing over the south of Britain. Any argument which holds good for the position of the objects in the Oban caves, or Oransay beaches, holds for them too. It looks as though the earliest boatmen belong to the second millenium B.C.

Here is an example of one of the great difficulties of archaeological research. There is a tendency to think that, because traces are found of a people living in one place and using a particular series of objects, that people must have lived there at about the same time that another group of people lived and used a similar series of objects somewhere else. It is not so at all. Ideas travel great distances and stick at the limits of their spread long after they have been superseded by later ideas nearer the centre of their origin. There may be four or six thousand years' interval in time between the Azilians of France and the cave-dwellers of Oban, yet some of their tools appear almost identical. Sword types evolved in central Europe about 600 B.C. remained in use in Africa till the last century. Brooches, apparently copied from those worn by Anglo-Saxon invaders of the seventh century A.D., are still worn in Scotland. It is by no means easy in archaeology to establish time scales which will hold good over wide areas. There must always be a time-lag in the spread of objects. Even such things as coins may take long years to spread. A Roman coin found in Islay may have taken fifty or a hundred years to get there from its minting place in the south.

If this idea of the period at which the Oban caves and the Oransay beach-dwellings were used is correct, it brings their former occupants into a story we already know something

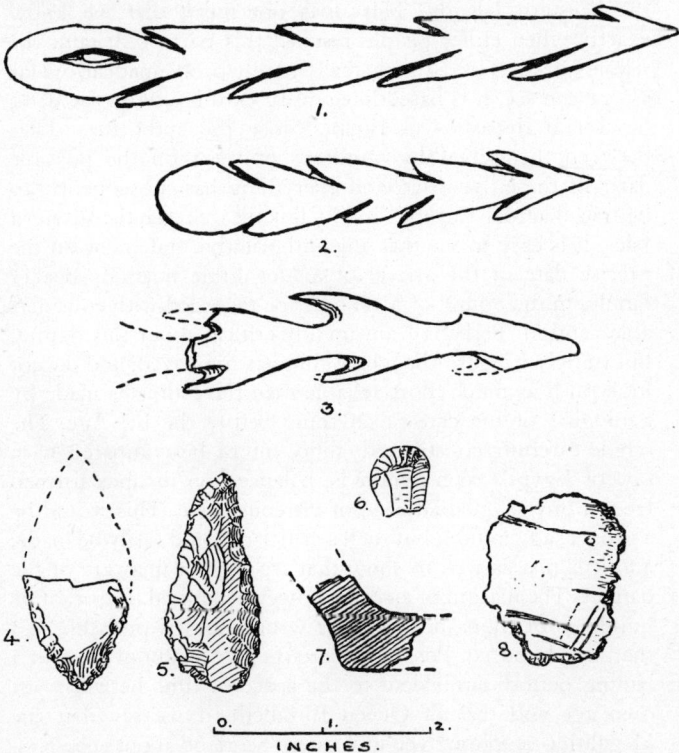

OBJECTS FROM THE '25 FOOT' RAISED BEACH

1 *and* 2. Bone barbs from the Oban caves (after Anderson).

3. Bone barb from Oransay (after A. Henderson Bishop). These are not harpoons but parts of bird-darts or laesters.

4. Broken flint arrow-head. 5. Flint knife. 6. Flint scraper. 7 and 8. Potsherds. 4—8 are from the Ardantrive rock-shelter. The shape of the base fragment, No. 7, is later than the Neolithic period and a date in the Early Bronze Age is probable for the occupation of this shelter.

about. These primitive fishing, shell-fish collecting and hunting people were more or less contemporary with the spread of Megalith builders and Early Bronze Age 'Beaker' people into the Western Islands. This does not mean that we know exactly when either people reached this part of Britain; the whole question of dating is really highly problematical. As far as one can see, it is based like a great card house on the dates of certain dynasties in Egypt. Since the authorities differ between themselves by hundreds of years on the possible dates of these dynasties, and everything has subsequently to be traced across Europe, link by link till we reach the Western Isles, it is easy to see that any authoritative statement on the precise date of the arrival of a Megalithic boat, or Beaker family, in the Sound of Mull must be regarded with considerable caution. Perhaps I am unduly critical about this dating, but frankly I regard the whole thing as unproved, and do not look on it as much more reliable than the estimates made by geologists of the date of anything before the Ice Age. The whole carefully constructed edifice might be compared with one of Egypt's own pyramids, balanced on its apex formed from a tiny segmented bead of vitreous paste. This would be a gross exaggeration, but such a criticism could easily be made, and it is just as well to show that we are not unaware of the danger. The margin of error is, however, limited. It cannot be hundreds of thousands of years wrong, and is probably less than five hundred. Possibly, therefore, we shall only be out a trifling period, equivalent to the space of time between our own age and that of Queen Elizabeth, if we say that the Megalithic people arrived in Western Scotland about 2000 B.C., and the Beaker people two or three hundred years later. Therefore it is quite reasonable to suggest that the people who occupied the Oban caves may have been living there about 2000 B.C.[3]

Perhaps I have laboured this point unduly, but, if care is not taken, we find the unproved theories of archaeologists creeping into history books, from which it is most hard to remove

them if they should prove wrong. Archaeology is still in its
teething stage; everyone makes mistakes in interpreting the
facts revealed by the spade. Completely new types of culture
are found from time to time, altering the whole conception of
the sequence of events. The danger is that a temporary stage
in the interpretation of the evidence may become a firmly
believed dogma before it has had a chance of being thoroughly
examined.

The late Sir William Ridgeway, when he was Disney
Professor of Archaeology at Cambridge, used to say, 'I trail
my coat before the young men till they learn to hit me. Then
they will begin to learn something.' Few archaeologists today
dare to trail their coats and it becomes blasphemous to
criticize the statements of a specialist. Let us try to follow
Ridgeway's example and risk making cockshies of ourselves.
A good shower of 'Irish confetti' will often serve to water the
field for the growth of learning. Ridgeway had another maxim
which I have found of value: 'Do not be like So-and-so, the
mere lickspittle of the German scholars'; in other words, 'let
us not be too sure that the published works of specialists on
the Continent are any more reliable than our own'. I had a
good example of this danger recently, when I was discussing
some problems of the Dark Ages with a celebrated Swedish
archaeologist. It transpired that they believed all we were
saying about the dating of certain styles of ornament, and we
were doing exactly the same by them. Neither group of
specialists had anything concrete to go on; it was anybody's
game.

The other great risk, which was pointed out by Dr. Glyn
Daniel in his *Three Ages*, is that of assuming a stage of culture
can be equated with an age. There is no reason to suppose that
in the days of Pytheas there were not groups of people living
in Britain in an Iron Age, a Bronze Age and a Stone Age.
This possibility was recognized years ago by Kipling in *The
Knife and the Naked Chalk*. But today, if you look at an
archaeological textbook, you get the impression of each age

succeeding the last with absolute regularity everywhere. This, of course, makes nonsense of the study of the past. Were not the chieftains of the Highlands in the fifteenth century depicted in armour like that worn by the English at Bannockburn, and did not the Irish earl appear at the beruffed and doubletted court of Queen Elizabeth in a pig-faced, bascinet helm? In earlier times, owing to the difficulties of communication in a country which was still largely covered by marsh and forest, not only tribes but individual communities would have been in very different stages of culture. A fishing community at Oban could be in the Stone Age, when one in Cornwall was ferrying tin for Massilia and another in Kent was smelting iron for sword blades. On the whole, however,

EFFIGY IN SKEABOST BURIAL GROUND, SKYE

The knight is clad in quilting and wears the Camail and Bascinet of the 14th century in England. His claymore is, however, of a much later date. There are several similar effigies in the West Highlands.

cultures appear to have spread in a remarkably uniform way over much of Britain. How long they took to spread is quite another matter, but I feel that, from the days of the Megalithic people onwards, there was much more movement by sea than anyone would have expected. Here I think it will be necessary to give some thought to geographical considerations

CHAPTER TWO

THE BRONZE AGE

I HAVE ALREADY MENTIONED the way in which the weight of the great ice sheet depressed the surface of the land in the north. These ice conditions were world-wide. The whole of the northern portions of the world were thus depressed, which naturally produced a compensating ring, or bulge, of land southward of the depressed area at a level higher than normal. How long it took, from the melting of these ice sheets until the land resumed its normal level, is very hard to judge, but it appears as if the process is not yet complete. A kind of gigantic see-saw has been slowly rocking ever since.

If we consider the effect of this, it becomes clear that enormous changes have taken place in the shape and topography of the world since the Ice Age. For a long period, southern Britain and France stood at a considerably higher level than they do now. A very large part of the bed of the North Sea was dry and fertile land. The coastline of France lay well to the westward of where it is today; the English Channel was quite narrow.

There were still islands in the North Sea in the days of Ptolemy, about 150 A.D., somewhere between the mouth of the Thames and Holland. These were the last vestiges of great tracts of land which appear for some centuries to have been the temporary breeding grounds of more than one migrant people, until the encroachments of the sea forced them to move outwards to east and west. Many years ago Sir Cyril Fox pointed this out to me as a new conception, but it is now quite generally accepted.

The North Sea people, who appear to have most influence on the future population of Britain, are known as the 'Beaker' men from their use of characteristic pottery drinking cups,

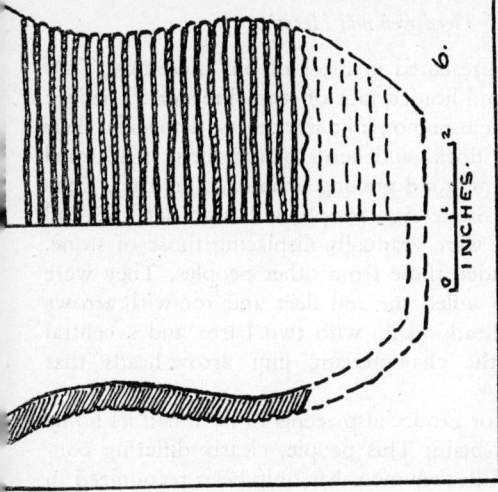

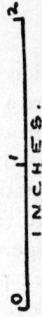

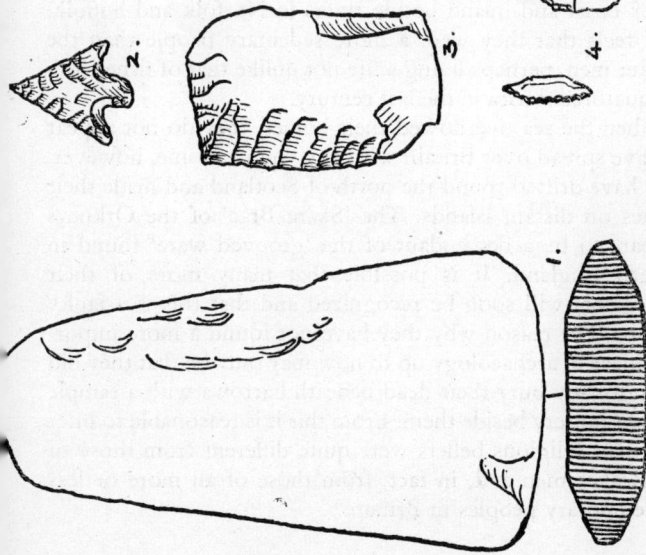

TYPICAL OBJECTS LEFT BY BEAKER MEN ON THEIR CAMP-SITES IN WESTERN SCOTLAND

1. Flat stone-axe influenced by early bronze forms.
2. Flint arrow-head as found on Ardnamurchan, Coll, the Uists, etc.
3. Flint knife.
4. Pigmy tools of Mesolithic type but found in the Islands with Beakers.
5. Pigmy flint scraper common all over West Scotland.
6. Cord-impressed 'B' Beaker found on Ardnamurchan and in Midlothian.

which are well represented in most of our museums. They were a sturdy, round-headed race of stock-breeders. I believe them at first to have been nomadic wanderers, who spent their lives driving their flocks and herds before them in seasonal migrations from one good grazing ground to another. They were essentially a Stone Age people, although flat axes and daggers of bronze were gradually displacing those of stone. They probably traded these from other peoples. They were also hunters, who killed the red deer and roe with arrows tipped with flint heads made with two barbs and a central tang; these are the characteristic flint arrow-heads that everybody knows.

A second tribe, or group, also seems to have had its home on the North Sea plain. This people, clearly differing considerably from the Beaker men, has only been recognized in recent years. They used a characteristic form of pottery, known at present by the unfortunate name of 'grooved ware'. Their settlements have been found below high-tide mark on the Essex coast and inland beside rivers in Norfolk and Suffolk. One feels that they were a more sedentary people than the Beaker men, perhaps living a life not unlike that of fisher-folk in equatorial Africa in the last century.

When the sea overflowed their homes, they do not appear to have spread over Britain with any vigour. Some, however, may have drifted round the north of Scotland and made their homes on distant islands. The 'Skara Brae' of the Orkneys appears to be a descendant of the 'grooved ware' found in eastern England. It is possible that many more of their settlements will soon be recognized and that this is a faulty picture. The reason why they have not found a more important place in archaeology up to now may only be that they did not normally bury their dead beneath barrows with a sample of their pottery beside them. From this it is reasonable to infer that their religious beliefs were quite different from those of the Beaker men and, in fact, from those of all more or less contemporary peoples in Britain.

It is usually believed today that the coming of the Beaker men to Britain occurred about 1800 B.C. They spread with some rapidity, for similar pottery vessels are found from the Outer Hebrides to Dorset or East Anglia. They spread, in fact, keeping their culture intact and unchanged. It is, of course, quite impossible to judge the rate of this spread. It may have taken one generation, or it may have taken hundreds of years. Many of them came to the east and north-east of Scotland, but quite a number spread to the western coasts and islands. They reached Argyll and the islands without first mixing with men of Neolithic culture, who were apparently there already. We must infer from this that they came in considerable numbers and in haste. The haste can hardly be due to anything other than the drowning of their former grazing lands by the sea. Some Beaker men appear to have reached western Scotland from Spain.

If this reasoning is correct, we must consider that the see-saw movement of the earth's crust was then in full swing, and that the highlands of Scotland were rising, while the coasts of England, France and even Spain were sinking. The beaches and caves of the twenty-five-foot raised beach sea may have emerged only recently to become habitable for men; or it may be that a still lower beach, which is visible in places just above the present high-tide mark, represents this stage of the see saw movement.

With the drowning of some coastlines and the rising of others, it is easy to see why all kinds of people were on the move in the search for new homes. Students of climatic changes appear to believe that at this period north-western Europe experienced a long age of continental climate, with prolonged easterly winds in summer and a sun heat comparable to that of Spain today. Coastal plains, river banks, sandy heaths, and relatively barren hill country would, therefore, be the only areas not supporting thick forest growth. Of necessity, movement would often have been water-borne.

Some people believe that much forest was deliberately

destroyed by fire to provide grazing and agricultural land. I
do not feel convinced that an oak forest could easily be burnt.
The undergrowth might be destroyed by fire, but to burn a
living oak is another matter. You cannot burn it when the sap
is up; would it ever be dry enough to burn in winter? I do not
doubt the correct observation of extensive fires noted by
continental scholars, but I feel it would probably be necessary
to fell the trees first, or perhaps bark them and leave them to
die, before they could be burnt. It would be a great labour to
clear even an acre of forest with a stone axe. But you could
destroy the undergrowth bit by bit, and leave your beasts to
eat the young trees as they appeared. In time the big trees
would die and you would have your cleared land. All the time
you could be nibbling at it, taking a tree here for a dug-out
canoe, one there for a new hut or a cattle pen. We are still left
with a picture of Britain utterly unlike the one we see today.

From the northern scarp of the Chilterns, along which the
droving way led for the seasonal migrations from Norfolk to
Salisbury Plain, Beaker man would look out over an unending
sea of trees, a blue and green ocean. No rising column of
smoke would probably be seen above its vast surface unless a
hunting party was out and roasting strips of venison over a
fire, or some fisher-folk were boiling a salmon on the bank of
a distant stream. Nothing would break its monotony but the
wheeling kites and the soaring buzzards. Behind him would
be another wall of trees stretching down to the Thames. As he
lay in the shade beneath a may bush or a juniper, he would
hear nothing but the lowing of his cows, the bleating of his
sheep, the barking of his dogs and the chatter of his women
and children, unless it was the far-off howling of a wolf, the
scream of a buzzard or the croaking of ravens hoping for
scraps, or carrion round his camp. This same picture could be
seen anywhere in the lowlands of Britain where man had
forced his way, except where the soil was too poor to support
forest growth. By the sea coasts and on the hills, however, it
was another story. In the heath-lands of East Anglia and the

Downs of Sussex industrial activity had already begun. Men were sinking shafts to mine flint and were bartering partly-fashioned axes. Soon in the west, men would be mining tin and copper, and in Ireland they would be panning for gold in the streams.

The other great movement of immigrants has, however, been left out of the picture, that of the Megalithic and Neolithic peoples. Perhaps they were all one people: no one really seems to know, although it seems probable that the branch, known as the Peterborough folk, had a North German Mesolithic ancestry.

When I first took up the study of archaeology, the Neolithic period covered everything from the close of the Ice Age to the Age of Bronze. Now it shrinks and contracts, year by year, and soon it will be divided up and will vanish altogether. Its earlier part has become Mesolithic, a period which hardly seems to concern northern Scotland at all, except in so far as some of its technicalities of stone-working appear to have been adopted by the Beaker men, and the men of the Oban caves and Oransay beaches were in a Mesolithic stage of culture. The rest of it is in process of division into 'As' and 'Bs' and 'Cs', which nobody can be bothered to remember, or, with more success, into Megalithic, or Windmill Hill, or Peterborough cultures. Perhaps it is easier to think of it as a time when men made huge stone tombs, round-bottomed pottery bowls and polished stone axes, and used barbless, leaf-shaped, flint arrowheads. In the west of England there was evidently war between the Beaker man and Megalithic man. They seem to have been of completely different racial stocks: the Beaker man with his round head, burly form, perhaps with blue eyes and fair hair, the Megalithic man with slight, delicate, oval face, long head, light frame, and probably brown eyes and dark hair. The Megalithic man had most elaborate religious beliefs and, like all seamen, was highly superstitious. He had to hide the entrances of his great communal temple tombs from violation by Beaker men. In

D

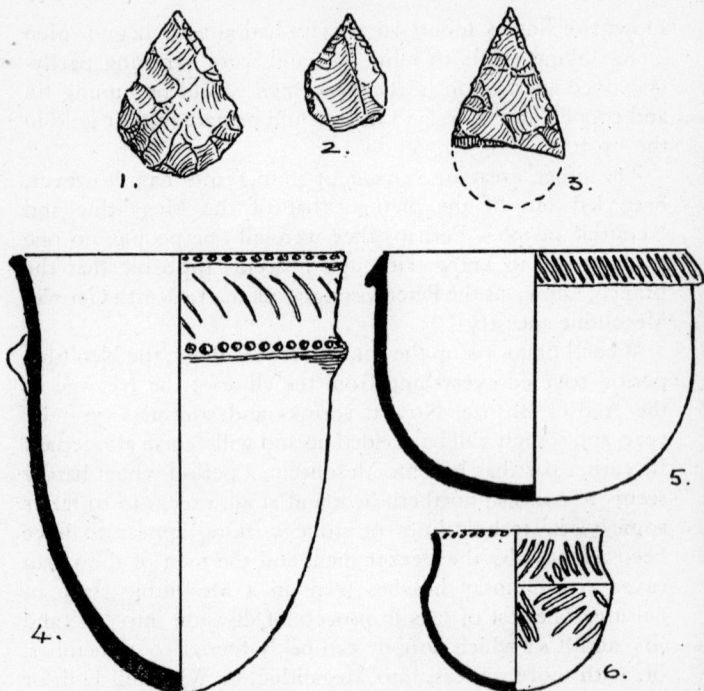

1—3.   Flint arrow-heads of Neolithic form from Western Scotland. The majority are small and roughly made owing to the scarcity of good flint. (No. 1 is 1 inch long.)

4—6.   Hebridean Neolithic pottery from Megalithic tombs.

4 *and* 6. From Clettreval, North Uist.

5.   From Rudh' an Dunzin, Skye (all after Lindsay Scott). (4 is 8½ inches wide at the mouth.)

The shape of an arrow-head is no certain guide for dating purposes. Leaf-shaped specimens have been found in Iron Age huts. The barbed and tanged form, however, does not appear to have come into use in Britain before the Beaker period. The wooden shaft of the leaf-shaped form extended almost to the tip and the purpose of the flint was only to enlarge the wound. Earlier forms, as with the Eskimos, probably consisted of small blades of flint set in the side of the shaft near the point. The function of a barbed arrow-head was clearly different. It was designed so that the arrow could not be drawn from the wound without detaching the head. The archer's quiver probably contained a variety of arrows for different purposes with different types of head.

Scotland the contacts were perhaps more friendly, and Beaker men were buried in the vaults of Langass Bharp or Clettreval in Uist and other places, with their characteristic arrowheads and pottery.

It seems that changes of climate and coastline, or perhaps pressure of population, caused extensive movements by sea up from the Spanish Peninsula to Britain, Ireland, and the islands to the northward. The origins of these peoples are still imperfectly understood, but there is no doubt that they were originally of Mediterranean stock, and settled among Neolithic peoples already here. They had some connexion with places as far away as Southern France, and even perhaps with Egypt itself. Their sea passage seems perilous today, when we think of the reputation of the Bay of Biscay; but, if the students of climate are correct, it was probably much less of an adventure than it appears to be. In prolonged easterly winds, boats could pass up the western shore of Europe in shelter. With so much land in the North Sea, there would be much less tide-water coming through the English Channel. The huge tides of the French coast probably did not become a problem till the North Sea was drowned. Then, of course, they must have seemed like a great rasp, ever widening their passage and tearing away great areas of land year by year. Megalithic voyagers to western Britain in summer may have had nothing better than dug-out canoes to transport them, but, if smugglers' gigs could make the passage to Brittany in the eighteenth century, with the ever-present risk of south westerly gales bringing in the full force of the North Atlantic, dug-outs could easily do so when the summer was almost certain to be calm. The story would be much the same right up to the Hebrides.

Of course the Megalithic people may not have used dug-out canoes. Their vessels may have been of hide-covered wicker-work, or real wooden boats built somewhat like those of ancient Egypt. In this connexion, as I have mentioned in earlier books, it is interesting to note that the Portuguese method of rowing today, with a wooden bull on the loom of the oar, which fits over a single thole pin in the gunwale, is the same as that employed by the curragh men of Ireland, and the river cobles of Scotland. Dug-out canoes, have, however, been found in considerable numbers on the Clyde in relation to the twenty-five-foot raised beach, and one is reported to have had a plug of cork.

At this early period, then, perhaps between 2000 and 1500 B.C., at least three peoples had reached and settled in the north and west of Scotland: the so-called Mesolithic people (Oban Azilians, etc.), the Neolithic (Megalithic, Peterborough, Windmill Hill, etc.), and the Beaker men. It is most unlikely that some of their descendants are not living there today. The Megalithic people were apparently the first grain culti-vators in Scotland.

It is difficult to get a clear picture of the real Bronze Age in Scotland. There is no dearth of antiquities. There are plenty of burials and numerous hoards of bronze objects. There are, as yet, no traces of settlements, with characteristic pottery and other relics of the cultures of the Age. But there are wooden idols, with the remains of wattled shrines, like the one found years ago beneath the peat beside Ballachulish ferry. All this is clear. The objects can be arranged in typological sequence. We can trace, especially at the beginning, imported bronze tools and axes from Ireland, or beads of so-called jet, or amber from abroad. What is not clear is whether any new peoples came in and settled there, or whether we are just observing the relatively simple evolution and coalescence of the three people whose immigration has already been briefly described.

The introduction of new types of sword or spear do not necessarily indicate the coming of a new people. The typical Beaker of early times appears to change gradually into a more complicated pot, known as a Food Vessel. This change seems to be due to a combination of the pottery fashions of the eastern and western immigrants. The great urns used for containing the ashes of the cremated dead, as well as for

ordinary domestic purposes, appear to go through a perfectly
natural course of evolution. The trouble lies in what I am
afraid we must regard as a most tiresome innovation. Everybody took to cremating their dead. I believe that this rite
began in a purely practical manner. The Beaker man's habit of
constructing great mounds over his dead relatives could only
be carried out when a large number of people were present.
If, therefore, somebody died when groups were all dispersed
to summer grazings and the like, it was necessary to preserve
the dead person in some way till the groups met together
again for seasonal migration.

It seems to me that this is the reason why so many con-
tracted skeletons are found in burials of the Beaker period and
Early Bronze Age. These skeletons I take to represent the
remains of persons who had been dried over a slow fire after
death. They were trussed up and smoked, and could then be
carried conveniently long distances on a pony, until the tribe
met together again. When they did meet, perhaps several
other groups had a similar dried mummy with them, and so
all were buried in one mound.

It is only a stage from this to complete cremation. Why not
burn the old man altogether? Then you could pick up the
ashes, put them in a pot and sling it in a pannier beside the
pony, with another pot full of cheese or skyr to balance it. In
time this would become a religious rite and all kinds of
reasons would be invented to explain the custom. You burned
the person so that his soul could fly away quickly and not be
earth-bound. Yes, but the whole point of the burial mound
and so on was to keep him earth-bound. The process shades
from inhumation to charred skeletons, and thus to complete
cremation. It began for convenience and ended as a rite. It
also helped in a modest way to clear the woodlands. It took a
lot of wood to make a good hot pyre. It cheered people up.
They danced round the fire and forgot their loss. It was
something to be encouraged for many reasons. It was much
nicer to look at a pot full of ashes, than at a grisly, dried face

grinning over the back of a pony. All the same, it is an inconvenience for archaeologists. There is no known way of restoring cremated bones, so that their shapes can be measured, and so it is impossible to say what the later Bronze Age people were like. The spread of cremation, however, to every corner of the British Isles does suggest that the various peoples already there were combining together to form a single race.

Other considerations suggest that large areas were under a central ruler. How else could you arrange for the transport of a complete sacred circle of stones from Prescelly Mountain, in Pembrokeshire, to Stonehenge in Wiltshire? The stones had to be dragged down to the sea: each one had to be slung perhaps between a pair of canoes, the flotilla had to be sailed, or paddled, round to the mouth of the Avon and quanted up the river; then the stones had to be dragged overland again and set up. This is a gigantic undertaking, and can only have been done on the authority of a great ruler, probably under pressure from his priests. It is just the same at the end of the Bronze Age, when the climate changed to the damp of the Atlantic weather-cycle. Peat grew rapidly in the lowlands of the Fens and Somerset, but somebody ordered the construction of elaborate and numerous corduroy and pile-driven roads, so that people could get to their grazings. These were not the work of a few villagers. Acres of wood and tons of sand went into their construction. They were executed under the orders of some great chief. This probably explains the uniform spread of many types of tools and weapons over wide areas of Britain. The country was organized in large units, probably right up to the Highland line. Whether these units were peacefully disposed towards each other, we may well doubt. The multitude of swords and spears were hardly carried for hunting or amusement. But it was good for the tin trade of Cornwall.

Long ago, Ridgeway suggested that the Ictis of Pytheas was the Vectis of the Romans, and that the tin was collected in the

Isle of Wight. If the central authority of much of Britain was in the neighbourhood of Stonehenge, as is suggested by the transportation of the Prescelly Stones, it may well be that Christchurch had become the port of entry for Cornish tin and that the use of Ictis was merely the survival of a long-accustomed practice; a case, in fact, of economic inertia.

There may be some confusion here between the port of export and the port of entry. The tin could indeed have been taken across to St. Michael's Mount in carts at low water, laden in curraghs which made a leisurely six days' coasting passage up Channel to Hengistbury Head, or some such place near Vectis, Ictis or Wight, whence it was sailed to Gaul in foreign ships of greater burthen. It was no longer in much demand in Britain, for the Bronze Age had given place to that of Iron in the southern districts. The great age of Celtic metal work had not yet begun.

The 'Wessex' culture, which is the somewhat anachronistic term used for a part of the Early Bronze Age in southern England, has yielded considerable evidence of trade with other countries. There are objects of Baltic amber and various small things, like model weapons, which have their counterparts in Central Europe. Of greater interest to our inquiry, however, are finds, particularly in Wiltshire, of quite a number of personal ornaments which clearly came from the eastern Mediterranean area. About twenty-five different graves have yielded small tubular and segmented *faience* beads, which were apparently made in Egypt about 1400 B.C. At the same time, a gold-and-amber disc has been found in a Wiltshire grave, which is exactly like one found in a late Minoan tomb in Crete. It may be thought that all these various objects can have come in by sea from the mouth of the Elbe, or some such port. It is, however, possible that they came by totally different routes.

The Megalithic people certainly came by the Western Ocean sea route: connexions between Ireland and the Iberian peninsula are clear enough for any archæologist to recognize.

We must examine the possibility that this route remained in use during the Bronze Age. We have already noted the importance of the trade in Cornish tin. Objects made of this metal have been found in the 'Wessex' culture graves. Early geographers knew that there were islands in the north-west, whence tin was obtained, but they were never certain whether these lay off the north-west corner of Spain, off the Breton peninsula, or even at a greater distance. This doubt is almost certainly due to the secretiveness of merchants, who feared for the safety of their markets. Phœnicians and Greeks were rivals for this trade.

Now Portugal can, I think, supply important clues in the solution of the problem. Several very ancient types of vessel are still in use there, in particular the wine-boats of Douro and the coastal sardine fishermen of the western seaboard. The barges of the Douro are now clinker-built, but they retain a most primitive shape of hull, and are steered by a helmsman standing on a raised platform, who operates an enormous sweep which swivels on the head of the stern-post. This method of steering has almost certainly survived in Portugal since the time of the twelfth dynasty in Egypt (*c.* 2100 B.C.). I do not say that it is of Egyptian origin; it may have come from anywhere in the Mediterranean. We do not know how much of the shipbuilding art of ancient Egypt was indigenous. It is known, however, that in earlier dynasties in Egypt, vessels were steered by two or more men operating paddles at the stern, and that in later times two quarter-rudders had been adopted. It looks as if the Douro type of steering sweep came to Portugal at about the time of the Early Bronze Age in Egypt, when it was popular in the latter country.

The Portuguese fishing-boats are even more remarkable. They are very beamy, flat-bottomed and carvel-built. Fortunately, they were well described by J. Guthrie in *The Mariner's Mirror* before they vanished from human eyes. These vessels, often fifty feet in length, are swept up at either end in great, unsupported curves. They are rowed by forty-

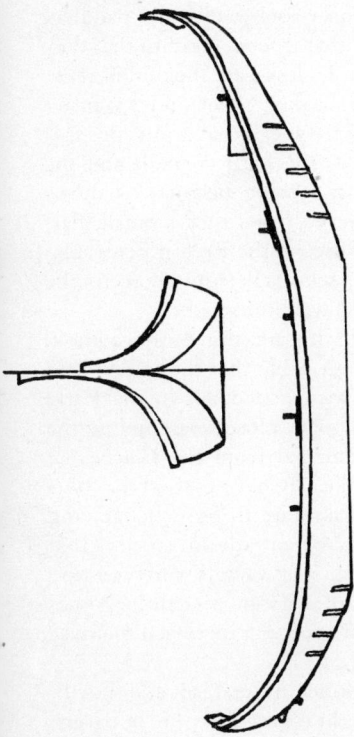

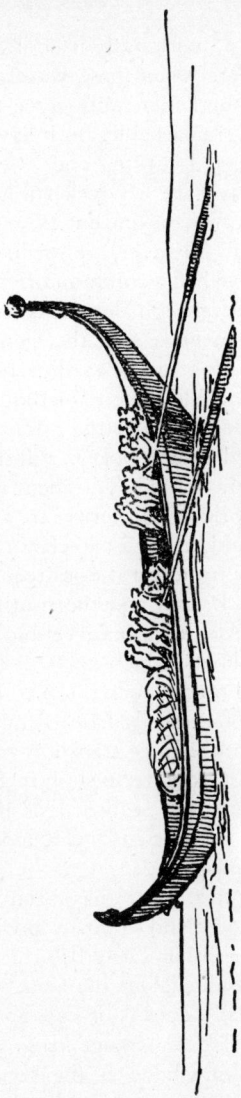

PORTUGUESE SAVEIRO

Length 55 feet

Plans after J. Guthrie. Drawing, based on photographs, to show method of rowing with sweeps 33 feet long. These vessels may resemble those used by Megalithic man and almost certainly do those of the British Bronze Age. The mop on the stem head goes back to the earliest representations of Phoenician ships in Ancient Egypt.

four men, working four enormous sweeps. They have no sail or rudder. When these vessels are compared with the model boats found in twelfth dynasty Egyptian tombs, the resemblance is remarkable. Both have the same flat bottoms and flat unsupported curving ends. Certain small details at stem and stern may have a Greek ancestry. The method of rowing is different, for the ancient Egyptian vessels were only paddled. The hulls, however, are so alike that it seems certain that they must have had a common origin. Unless I am much mistaken, the Irish curragh developed its broken sheer and swept-up bow from vessels of this general type. I have already said that the Portuguese sardine boat, the Irish curragh and the Scottish coble have a method of rowing peculiar to themselves. It is interesting to observe, too, that a small, flat-bottomed fishing boat is still in use on the Breton peninsula. The dories of the Terraneuvas, who sail from there to the New World cod fisheries, are also flat-bottomed.

It would be unwise to elaborate this question until we know more about it, but it does seem probable that the trade in tin between Britain and the south was carried out in the Early Bronze Age in large carvel-built boats, closely resembling the sardine boats which are still launched from the beaches of Portugal today. Such boats could easily have carried the 'blue stones' of Prescelly from Pembrokeshire to Stonehenge, and all this problem of transport may be entirely imaginary. It is perhaps reasonable to suppose that such vessels were working up the western seaboard of Europe from Megalithic times until the climatic change of about 1000 B.C. increased the risks of the passage.

Very little work has been done in western and north-western Scotland to throw any light on the daily life of people in the Neolithic–Early Bronze Age phase. Many burials have been examined, but the actual settlement sites await excavation. Small clachans of Late Stone Age houses in the Orkneys have, for some strange reason, been regarded by Professor V. Gordon-Childe as the homes of primitive communists.

It is far more probable that these are the dwellings of single families living in a matrilineal, and probably matriarchal, system. As each daughter married, she brought her husband to the house settlement, where they added a new hut to the group. The whole community was probably lashed into unwilling activity by the bitter tongue of a toothless old grandmother. 'Stop gnawing those mutton bones in the bed, Colin, and get out to keep the ravens off the lambs'. It is of interest, however, in these Orkney settlements, to see the overwhelming evidence of an almost completely pastoral existence. Sheep and cattle were the life of the people. Spindly-legged sheep and little cows, like those of western Ireland today, occupied the greater part of the lives of the men in northern and western Scotland. Much the same story is probably true of the men of the Beaker settlements on the machair grazings of Ardnamurchan, or Uist, which were undoubtedly more extensive than they are today. The Beaker man was, however, a great hunter too. His arrowheads and the tiny 'Tardenoisean' barbs of his bird-darts, or laesters, are common all over the west coast. When, and on what terms, he merged with the Neolithic people is not yet known.

A picture of north-western and western Scotland during the period of continental climate should not be hard to form. Inland, and probably extending right up into Sutherland, lay the great woods. Blankets of peat had not begun to grow: even the islands were wooded. The fierce gales from the western ocean did not sweep far inland, to burn up the vegetation with their salt breath, as they do today. These woodlands were still extensive right down to the days of Queen Elizabeth. In the Bronze Age they must have been an impassable barrier to the spread of settlement. The coastal plains were, however, more extensive than they are now, and formed a fertile belt on the west, extending in some cases a great distance beyond the present limits. Sheep and cattle could be supported in considerable numbers, not only on them, but in the lighter woodlands behind them. Small semi-wild cattle grazed in these woodlands till the days of the Georges. Along these coastal plains Beaker and Megalithic man, Neolithic and Mesolithic, all met and mingled. By the middle of the Bronze Age there was probably no real distinction between any of them, except where groups became isolated, as in Orkney, through the gradual decay of the Irish trade routes. These routes may well have dated back to before the drowning of the North Sea plains. Megalithic man could probably reach Denmark by hugging the coasts all the way round the west, north and east of Scotland.

In the earliest Bronze Age there appears to have been much trade across and round the north of Scotland with the metal workings of Ireland. Bronze and gold objects made in Ireland are found in some numbers, not only in Scotland, but in Denmark and the neighbouring countries. At the present time, some scholars think that the Irish bronze-workers had control over the working of tin in Cornwall. Later on this control appears to have been lost, and the monopoly of the tin trade passed into the hands of the peoples living in England. This seems a most plausible suggestion, and accounts for the widespread distribution of early Irish gold work and other objects, which appears to have been largely discontinued in the later part of the Bronze Age. It also accounts for the relative poverty of western Scotland after the early Bronze Age. It no longer lay on an important trade route. This route may not have been much used again till the days of the Vikings. It is improbable that traffic between Scotland and Ireland was ever wholly suspended, but there was no longer a brisk passage of vessels from Ireland, through the Sound of Mull and Kyles of Skye, round Cape Wrath and through the Pentland Firth, and onward over the North Sea. Even in the calm summer weather of a Continental climate, this seems an adventurous journey for a dug-out canoe, with its low freeboard and general lack of stability. It looks more like a task for a big curragh, or a built boat. Perhaps one of these vessels will be eventually found beneath an Irish or Scottish peat moss.

It is clear that the idea of a dug-out boat originated in the woodlands of the south, and was probably suggested by the partly charred trunk of a tree. The origin of the skin boat, however, must be quite different. It must, I think, be the earlier type, and may even go back to the days of Palæolithic hunters. The present distribution of skin boats in the Arctic, in Ireland, in Wales and Tibet probably only marks the survival, in scattered places, of what was once an almost world-wide vehicle of transport.

There is little doubt as to the general routes taken by the early Bronze Age merchants, as far as Britain is concerned. One clearly went by sea from northern Ireland into the Clyde. There goods were taken ashore and carried to the Forth, from whence they were taken by sea to the Danish peninsula. A second route passed from northern Ireland up the Firth of Lorne, and from the beaches about Fort William packages of halberds and daggers were carried up the Great Glen to the neighbourhood of Inverness, where they were loaded once more for the North Sea voyage. The third route was north-about through the Pentland Firth. Irish bronzes and gold went by these routes outward from Ireland; Baltic amber came back again. Quite a reasonable quantity of the bronzes and gold remained in Scotland. It is interesting to note that an appreciable number of Irish gold objects have been found in the Lorne district. The bracelets from near Onich are well-known. The nearby find of the female wooden idol may be an indication that Onich itself was a place where goods were landed for the porterage. Here perhaps thanks were offered for the success of the first part of the expedition, and dues were paid for the hire of porters for the next lap. It is interesting to observe that these wooden idols are found in Denmark, as well as Scotland, England and Ireland. Some have thought them to be of Viking origin, but they are found beneath the later peat, which we now think began to form towards the end of the Bronze Age, when the climate changed from the Continental type to one more like that of today, but even wetter.

Irish bronzes reached the Portree district of Skye and even the Outer Hebrides. Among the ideas which returned was that of the stone axe, with a central hole for the haft. A peculiar form of this, a ceremonial axe-hammer with an exaggerated waist at the socket, is found from Ireland round by the Orkneys to Slesvig, where it occurs as charms on amber necklaces. That this represents an idea brought back from the east, and not a traffic in goods, is evident from the fact that the Scottish and Irish axes are made from local stone. One of the Orkney axes was found in a cist grave with a cremation showing that it was of relatively late date.

Enough has now been said to show that in early Bronze Age times, perhaps up to about 1200 B.C., men were moving about all over the west coast of Scotland in boats which could face the crossing of the North Sea. They could navigate well enough to make voyages for days out of sight of land. These seamen could certainly have made the passage to Thule had they wished to do so. The possibility of finding some traces of Bronze Age man in Iceland cannot be ruled out, but, if they are found at some future date, we must expect them to be limited to such things as flint arrow-heads, scrapers, or axes. A small stone cist might possibly be found if somebody died up there. An empty cist was actually found many years ago on the island which forms part of Reykjavik harbour. There is no proof of the age of this cist, but some day one may turn up with its contents intact. I am sorry for the future discoverer of Bronze Age objects in Iceland, and hope he is a chewer of tobacco.

The Bronze Age probably supported a more or less uniform way of life for hundreds of years. The latter part of it was marked by a nearly complete cleavage between the peoples of the west and north from those of the south and east. Land routes to the south extended the culture of southern Britain right round to the Moray Firth and to the Clyde. The north and west, however, although remaining in contact with Ireland, were more or less cut off from this stream of culture.

The reason may perhaps be sought in the Irish loss of control of the Cornish tin. They could no longer export bronze at a profit across the width of Scotland and the North Sea. Gold too may have been becoming increasingly hard to win from the workings. Western Scotland entered a period of increasing isolation from the main culture movements of the western world, but, on top of this, there came something of a more drastic nature, which must have had a profound effect on the lives of everybody.

Somewhere about 900 B.C. and again perhaps about 600 B.C. the students of climate notice a sharp swing from Continental to Western Ocean weather. This change, according to the theories of von Post and others, was world-wide. It set people moving everywhere, for those who had been living at the limit of cultivation and were dependent on the dry warm summer for their slender harvests could no longer support life when the summer became cold and wet. These wet periods may only have lasted a short time, but their results were to last for ever. Hungry tribes fought their way south in search of land to live on: tribe pushed out tribe. The whole of Europe began to move. Movements, originated by climatic changes, continued long after the wet periods were over. France, with her weak strategic frontiers on the east, was overrun again and again by wandering peoples. It was like throwing a stone at a pane of glass; splinters flew in every direction. It is clear that the first movements of displaced tribes into Britain began soon after the climatic change; but, as the climatic change is dated from the stratification of archaeological material, the dating depends on archaeology.

The first peoples to come into Britain were in a late stage of Bronze Age culture and are known as 'Urnfield' men. They had probably been pushed out of their North German homes by invaders from the north. These Urnfield men are thought to be the first Celts to settle in Britain, and to have been followed, some hundreds of years later, by similar immigrants, who had already learnt the use of iron. As far as can be judged

at present, bands of immigrants flooded the whole of Britain
from different directions, and in time penetrated the whole of
Scotland. Britain became a land ruled by Celtic- or proto-
Celtic-speaking warriors. They appear to have called it something like Alba, Alban or Albion. Much warfare must have
taken place at this time. It is possible that broken elements of
the earlier bronze-using peoples may have sailed away in
disgust and attempted to live in Iceland: others pushed into
Ireland. These events could have caused the sailing to Thule
of which Pytheas speaks. Thule could certainly have supported
their sheep and some of their cattle; men still transport
trussed-up cows in curraghs from the Irish islands to the
mainland. Or was this sailing carried out by entirely different
people? Was it carried out by men from Denmark or Norway,
in ships like those depicted in the Scandinavian rock engrav-
ings, and is this why Pytheas continued his travels in that
direction? Some people think he sailed far into the Baltic;
others think that he only reached the mouth of the Elbe, but
he certainly did go eastwards. Can we perhaps picture him
busy with his solar observations in Shetland, when a shipload
of trappers pulled in to break their voyage on the way to
Thule? Strange but genial men they might have been, in a
strange vessel with long curving bifid stem and stern, part
dug-out and part ship. All seamen find ways of communicating
together, even if they know no single word of each other's
languages. They point to an oar, or sail, or brace, and tell their
name for it with a grin. The others reply with their word. It
does not take long before they are talking.

Archaeology then, cannot at present tell us who was sailing
to Iceland three hundred years before the birth of Christ. It
can, however, point to people who might have gone there,
and give a background against which future possible discoveries may be studied. In the next chapter, I will try to paint a
picture in which archaeological evidence for northern voyages
already exists.

Up to this point in the story, there is not the slightest

evidence that any racial element entered the south of Britain and did not work its way up into Scotland also. The possible exception is Palæolithic man.

It is, in fact, a point of interest that, in spite of national propaganda, which has for centuries made out that the Scotsman is different from the Englishman, it is quite clear that both races are, in fact, made up of the same constituent elements, although the actual proportions of those elements may differ. Throughout the long period of perhaps four thousand years in which we are able to study the gradual building up of the national stocks, there does not appear to be a single breed of man which settled in England and did not do so in Scotland also. The units are, in fact, too large to be distinguished. There is more difference between the average collection of men in a Highland area in Scotland and an average collection in the Lowlands, than there is between a Lowland group and one in the Midlands of England. There can be no such thing as a typical Scotsman or a typical Englishman. There is, however, a definite break along the edge of the mountain mass of the Highlands. Beyond this line no settlements of Saxon immigrants were made. The Highlander, like the Welshman, appears to be almost free from teutonic blood, except that which came from Norseman and Norman. It may be possible to speak of a typical Highlander, but he must be chosen from districts in the centre of the mountain mass.

I mention this because the 'average', or 'typical' Scotsman may be shown to us at any moment now. The 'average' Englishman is already on view. I was shown his head a year or two ago. The head was a great surprise at first; I thought the whole thing was a joke, till I saw how serious the anthropologist was who was showing it to me. I have excavated hundreds of Anglo-Saxon graves and the general shape of their skulls is well-known to me. The 'average' Englishman was something quite different. He had a very long thin skull and an enormous nose; he had probably been a little dark man, with an anxious

E

face and beady black eyes. 'How on earth did you find the average?' I asked. 'Oh, by measuring ten thousand skulls from the old London grave-yards' was the answer. Then I saw what had happened. It was just as if you had measured all the dogs in Mayfair, and taken the average as being a typical English dog. All the sheep-dogs of the hills, all the setters, pointers, retrievers, fox-hounds, and the rest, would have been left out. London was never a true Saxon settlement; it was a cosmopolitan port for nearly two thousands years. To its Romano-British population were added generations of foreigners of every kind, and also generations of skilled craftsmen, who are frequently of the Mediterranean type. The 'average' Englishman, who is probably firmly installed in the text-books by this time, is an average Londoner of before the Industrial Revolution. You are not likely to meet him pitching turnips into a cart, or picking herrings out of a drift net. You may find him behind the counter of your bank, but you will not find him tramping round his hill sheep with his dog. When the 'average' Scotsman comes along, we shall probably recognize him as a Clydebank Irishman.

CHAPTER THREE

MEN OF THE BROCHS AND GALLIC WALLS

THE NEXT PERIOD of British history, the Early Iron Age, is
most complicated. This is partly due to the fact that traditions
have been preserved which relate to it, but which are difficult
to interpret. The old Irish heroic stories make frequent
mention of peoples who lived in Scotland, of whom the most
interesting for our study are the Fomorians, who apparently
lived on the West Coast and in the Islands. It is not necessary
to go into great details here. The reader can study H. M.
Chadwick's *Early Scotland*, where he will find the matter
discussed.

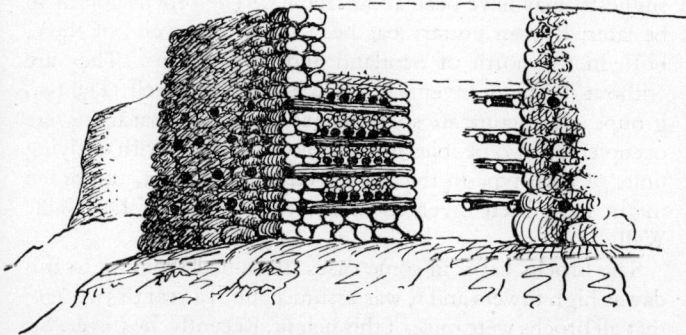

SCHEMATIC RESTORATION OF GALLIC WALL FORT

*The walls were bonded together with heavy oak timbers at about three foot
intervals. Other timbers were laid across these and the gaps filled with rubble. It
was suggested by Dechelette that once these logs became ignited the gaps between the
stones would serve as flues and enough heat would be generated to fuse the rubble core
of the walls if the stones were of suitable character. Gordon-Childe proved this to be
the case experimentally. Vitrified Forts are Gallic Wall forts which have been
burnt. The burning was probably caused by setting fire to the roofs of huts built
against the inner side of the wall. Iron arrow-heads for carrying burning material
have been found on Roman fort sites in Scotland.*

From the archaeological point of view, the problem resolves itself into two questions: (1) Who built the stone forts, often destroyed or slighted by fire, and known as 'vitrified'; and (2) Who built the brochs?

The forts were constructed with timber tie-beams in a manner well-known in Gaul, and are consequently described as of murus-gallicus construction. Several of them have produced brooches, which are thought to have gone out of use on the Continent about 250 B.C. No Roman pottery has been found in any of them, and they may have been stormed by Agricola's legions, or in inter-tribal warfare at an earlier date. The dating is discussed in Childe's *Scotland Before the Scots*. Chadwick thinks that the builders of the murus-gallicus forts were Welsh-speaking Gauls, invading the east of Scotland by sea without passing up through England first. The date of this invasion, which almost certainly took place as Chadwick suggests, may have been about 200 B.C. The brochs appear to be later; Roman pottery has been found in several of them, both in the north of Scotland and in the south. They are without doubt an invention made in Scotland itself. The two groups of structure are so located as to suggest that they were occupied by two peoples hostile to one another, with outlying units of each type in the other's territory. In fact, the broch might have been invented to meet the threat of the Gallic Wall.

The brochs have, in some cases, remained standing to this day as high towers and it was assumed, until a year or two ago, that all brochs were once of this height. Recently, however, Sir Lindsay Scott has suggested that most of them were merely stone walls enclosing a low, beehive-shaped farm-house. I think myself that a large number of brochs were probably high towers, but that others were simply round fortified farm-houses, protected by a parapet walk. I have no doubt at all that they were evolved from round, stone-walled houses, and that their purpose was tactical security and not aggression. The people who lived in them were farmers, but they lived in

days of peril and went about their daily tasks with their spears
in their hands. But who were they? Their pottery, which is
coarse and bad, is taken by Scott to have been derived from
that of the Veneti of the Breton peninsula, whose ships and

RECONSTRUCTION OF A BROCH TOWER

*This combines features observed in several surviving towers. The Broch of Mousa
in Shetland is still 40 feet high. Others were probably lower and many may never
have exceeded two storeys in height. 'Wheel-houses' appear to have been similar in
general principles but of only one storey and with the posts replaced by stone piers.*

*There was probably no smoke vent in the roof for the draught from the entrance
passage would force the smoke up the spiral staircase and out through the hollow
walls.*

towns were destroyed by Julius Cæsar. I feel myself that the
ceramic evidence is not strong enough to be convincing.
There may have been some Venetic settlers among the broch
builders, but I think that the pottery, and such household

objects as have survived, are more in keeping with peoples from southern Britain who were being driven from their homes by the Belgic invasion, which had perhaps begun a generation before Cæsar scourged the Veneti. I can see great resemblances between the culture of the broch people and those of various pre-Belgic Iron Age settlers from Cornwall to Cambridgeshire and Yorkshire. I feel that the broch people were parts of tribes in southern Britain, who, finding themselves too weak to beat off the Belgæ, decided to seek new homes in the north. They could not settle in south and east Scotland, for it had been recently occupied by continental Gauls of much the same stock as themselves; but they could overcome the earlier peoples of the north and west. Here they settled at their peril and here they evolved their defended farm-house. The southern brochs may be the earliest, and not off-shoots from the northern mass. Some pieces of broch pottery were found at Traprain Law, near the mouth of the Forth, in the hill town of a different people and at an early level.

As far as I can see, some brochs were in use right into the Dark Ages. I very much doubt whether their position was ever strategic, as Professor Chadwick thought. The isolated group in Galloway may represent an attempt at settlement which was frustrated by the tribes already in possession. This question cannot be cleared up till many more brochs have been excavated. We are only guessing at present. There is one detail, however, which I feel points strongly to the broch builders being quite different from the Veneti. The Veneti were builders of large wooden ships. The brochs are seldom anywhere near a suitable harbour for such vessels. They are the homes of farmers, who, if they used a boat, probably went cuddie fishing in a curragh. A seafaring people may change to farming, but it will not completely change the construction of its boats. A Venetic settler would build an oaken vessel, if he wanted a boat at all. If there are traces of Venetic settlement, they may be the promontory forts at such places as Loch Ainort in Skye.

Here perhaps it is convenient to mention the geographical work of Ptolemy, about 150 A.D. There are many texts of his geography, some in Greek and some in Latin; all are to some extent distorted by time and by the hands of the copying scribes. They take the form of lists of places, with their latitude and longitude beside them, and there are still in existence medieval maps which are thought to be copies of maps Ptolemy drew. There are errors of all sorts, both in maps and texts, but there is a large residue of fact which is of the greatest interest and value. Many places recorded by Ptolemy bear almost the same names today. The localities of tribes are recorded with their towns. In some cases we find that these tribal names in Scotland are repeated in southern Britain. The Cornavii or Cornovii of Caithness, an area of many brochs, have the same name as the occupants of Cornwall and Devon. The Damnonii or Dumnonii of the district round the head of the Clyde are found again near the Welsh border. We get the impression of portions of tribes being forced out in different directions by an invading people. This invading force was almost certainly Belgic.

The broch people settled in fortified farms all over Orkney and Shetland. They do not appear to have colonized the Faeroe Islands, but here once again is a time when men could have been constrained to make the passage over the sea to Iceland. There is no evidence that they did so. Had they done so, there would have been no need for them to construct brochs. Their farms would have been of the wheel-house type, associated with the broch culture in Scotland. Certain forms of modern Icelandic sheep-fold are not unlike wheel-houses, but the resemblance is probably superficial. It may seem foolish to make frequent mention of possible visitors to Iceland, but, in view of Pytheas' report, the connexion between Scotland and Iceland may have been much more pronounced than anyone has yet thought.

One curious feature about the culture of the broch, or wheel-house, people should be mentioned here. In North Uist

■ = Area dominated by 'Broch' people.

✕ = Area dominated by 'Gallic Wall' people.

ORCADES

NABARUS

CÆRENI

CORNAVII

TARVEDRUM

LUGI

ILA

CARNONACÆ

SMERTÆ

DECANTÆ

VARAR

LOXA

CERONES

CALEDONII

VACOMAGI

TEZALI

DEVA

TAVA

MALAEUS

CREONES

EPIDII

DAMONII

VENICONES

BODERIA

ÆBUDES

LONGUS

CLOTA

OTADINI

SELGOVÆ

EPIDIUM

RERIGONIUS

NOVANTÆ

BRIGANTES

considerable use was made of mattocks formed from the bones
of whales, which appear to be identical with mattocks used by
early Eskimos to flense blubber from whales. The possibility
cannot be wholly excluded that Eskimos in umiaks were blown
eastward across the North Atlantic. There are two objections
to this idea; the first is that archaeologists studying the cultures
of the Eskimo have not observed any traces of them in Greenland at such an early period; the second is a doubt whether the
crews of such umiaks, unprepared for the voyage, could have
survived the passage. It may be that these blubber-mattocks
are the idea of a much earlier race than the broch people, who
survived in the Hebrides down to this period and merged
with them. Some of the tools used by the people in the
Orkneys have a certain look of Eskimo objects. A form of
stone ulo blade, for instance, is common round the north of
Scotland and is spoken of as a Pict's knife. On the whole, it
seems probable that these cultural traits are survivals from an
extensive Mesolithic sub-Arctic culture, which left harpoons
and the heads of bird-bolts in Scandinavia. These problems will
have to be solved in the future. It is curious, for instance, that
the Lappish winter house of turf, which is by no means unlike
the old Eskimo long-house of Greenland, should be called a
'gamme'; while the underground storehouse of the Early Iron
Age in Scotland, with its long subterranean passage, is known

---

THE RELATIVE DISTRIBUTION OF BROCH AND
GALLIC WALL PEOPLES IN SCOTLAND

The names of tribes as given by Ptolemy and also some of his place
names are shown.

*It seems as if the Cornauii, Lugi, Cæreni and Carnonacæ were certainly Broch
people. If the Cerones (or Creones) represent Ptolemy's attempt to write Cruithnigh
then it seems that the Cruithnigh (or Picts) were a Gallic Wall people. It is
probable that the islands of 'Sketis' and 'Dumna' of Ptolemy are Skye and The
Lewis but their position is badly displaced in his work.*

*The area occupied by the Gallic Wall people is almost the same as that of the
men of the later Bronze Age who used cinerary urns for their burials. The Gallic
Wall people however seem to have occupied rather more of the west including the
Great Glen, Kintail, Morven and Islay.*

SEE ILLUSTRATION ON OPPOSITE PAGE

as a 'uamh' or 'weem'. Why is the Indian skin tent known also as a 'wig-wam'? Are these all traces of a former circum-polar language? Are these just infantile guesses, or did the Magdalenian hunter stagger back under the weight of an ibex to the door of his 'wam'.

Before we leave the broch people, there is one more

---

1. Horn Harpoon from Tara, Co. Down (after E. E. Evans and C. Hawkes). This has had a stone point. It may be a genuine Eskimo specimen but exact parallels are hard to find. (2½ inches long.)
2. Horn Harpoon without stone point but of same general type. I excavated this from a hut of the Arctic Whaling Culture in North East Baffin Land. Compare also the specimen (No. 11) from Ellesmere Land on page 124.
3 & 4. Whale-rib Mattocks. From an earth-house with Broch pottery at Foshigarry, North Uist (after Beveridge). (3 is 17 inches long.)
5. Whale-rib Mattock from North Devon Island. I excavated this specimen from an eskimo hut of the Arctic Whaling Culture. (Mattocks probably used for turf cutting as well as flensing whales.)
6. Walrus tusk Mattock from Ipiutak, Alaska (after Larsen and Rainey). Probably about the same date as the numerous Foshigarry specimens.
7 & 8. A pair of 'jet' labrets or ear-studs from Yorkshire (after Mortimer).
9. One of the earliest known Eskimo labrets from Ipiutak, Alaska (after Larson and Rainey). Same scale as the harpoons.
10. Bone Harpoon (Stone Age) from Skibshelleren, Norway (after J. Bøe).

The Eskimos till recent years continued to wear a pair of labrets of stone or ivory in the lower lip. Similar studs of jet or lignite are sometimes found in British burials of the earlier Bronze Age. It is uncertain however how long the practice continued. A recently discovered burial at Chesterford in Essex was provided with one of these studs. It is believed to have been buried through the floor of a ruined Romano-British building (information from Major Brinson who excavated the skeleton).

The three harpoons from Ireland, Norway and Baffin Land were clearly used in exactly the same manner with a lashing round the open socket for the harpoon foreshaft. The harpoon became detached in the body of the animal which was struck by it and a line through the central perforation prevented the escape of the quarry (probably a seal).

It is hard to account for these various cultural similarities which include other things ranging from cantilever house construction to the shape of pins without assuming either the spread of a former culture right round the northern hemisphere or actual contact by sea at some later time. Many parallels between the culture of the Eskimo and that of the palaeolithic Magdalenians of France are to be found in Sollas' 'Ancient Hunters'.

SEE ILLUSTRATION ON OPPOSITE PAGE

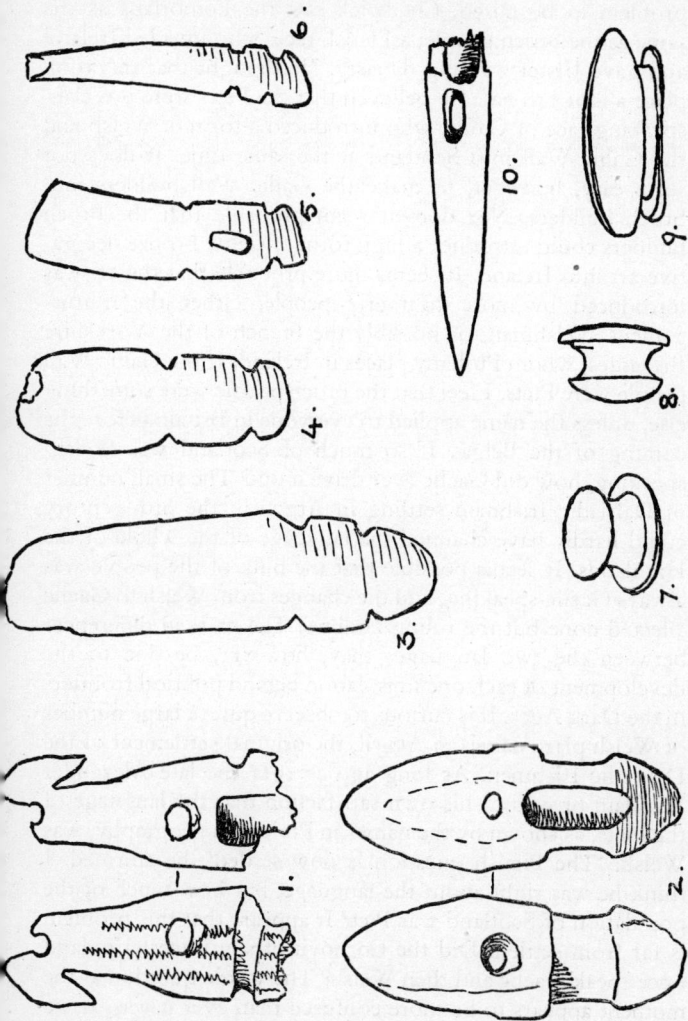

SOME ESKIMOID OBJECTS FROM THE BRITISH ISLES, ETC.

problem to be raised. Chadwick saw the Fomorians as the
same as the broch people; a Pictish race, who invaded Ireland
and gave Ulster a ruling dynasty. He thought that this took
place about 150 B.C. He believed that the Picts were a Welsh-
speaking race of Gauls, who introduced a form of Welsh and
the Gallic Wall into Scotland at the same time. It does not
seem easy, however, to make the Gallic Wall builders into
broch builders. Nor does it seem probable that the broch
builders could introduce a high form of Celtic bronze decorative art into Ireland. It seems more probable that the art was
introduced by more southerly people; either the murus-
gallicus Welshmen, or possibly the branch of the Yorkshire
Brigantes, whom Ptolemy places in Ireland. If the Gallic Wall
people were Picts, I feel that the broch people were something
else, unless the name applied to everyone in Britain before the
coming of the Belgæ. If so much of Scotland was Welsh-
speaking, how did Gaelic ever drive it out? The small number
of Dalriadic Irishmen settling in Argyll in the fifth century
could hardly have changed the language of the whole of the
Highlands. It seems possible that the bulk of the people was
always Gaelic-speaking, and the changes from Welsh to Gaelic
affected none but the ruling families. The marked differences
between the two languages may, however, be due to the
development of each one in isolation behind political frontiers
in the Dark Ages. It is curious to observe quite a large number
of Welsh place names in Argyll, the original settlement of the
Dalriadic Irishmen. As long ago as 1911 the late Alexander
MacBain proved to his own satisfaction that the language of
the Picts, as shown by the names in Ptolemy's geography, was
Welsh. 'The Pictish question is now settled', he affirmed. I
think he was right about the language, but how much of the
population of Scotland was Pict? It appears that this problem
is far from settled. Did the Cornovii of south-west England
once speak Gaelic and then Welsh? The whole question at the
moment appears to be more confused than ever it was. If we
look at it as archaeologists, we see a Gaulish people arriving

and building their forts over half of Scotland. Soon after, a second people, coming perhaps from the south of Britain, occupy the other half with fortified farms. Both races are thought to have spoken Welsh, and yet all the descendants of the second group, some perhaps coming from Cornwall, a district that was Welsh-speaking two hundred years ago, speak Gaelic. To add to this, we get Welsh place names in the only district known to have been directly colonized from Ireland, and no one has ever doubted that the Irish were Gaelic speakers.

The only explanation of the language problem which appears to make any sense to me, is that the Welsh-speakers were few in number, and that Gaelic was spoken over most of Britain before they came. There are probably Megalithic, Neolithic, Beaker-man, and even Mesolithic and Palæolithic words in Gaelic today, as well as French, Norse, Latin, Anglo-Saxon and Flemish. In any case, it does not look as if the historical events can be explained by a study of language, but rather that the language problems may be understood when the historical events have been ferreted out. The same thing appears true with regard to Anglo-Saxon settlement in Britain. The linguistic tail has a tendency to try to wag the historical dog.

I am doubtful whether the broch and wheel-house people settled in the Hebrides as early as at present is believed. It also seems as if their cultural elements were very mixed before they got there. The pottery, which Scott thinks to be the earliest, has the look of a mingling of ceramic ideas drawn from the Iron Age pre-Belgic peoples of southern Britain, with late Bronze Age pot forms known as encrusted urns. Along with this pottery are found iron ring-headed pins, of a type common in the first and second centuries A.D. at Traprain Law, and also bone pins with Ball, Baluster and Collared heads, whose shapes appear to have been derived from the types of Roman Britain. It is not easy to see how these men could have been the same as the Formorians. The Formorians may have been in a late Bronze stage of culture. It is, however, uncertain whether the pottery is the earliest kind made by the broch people.

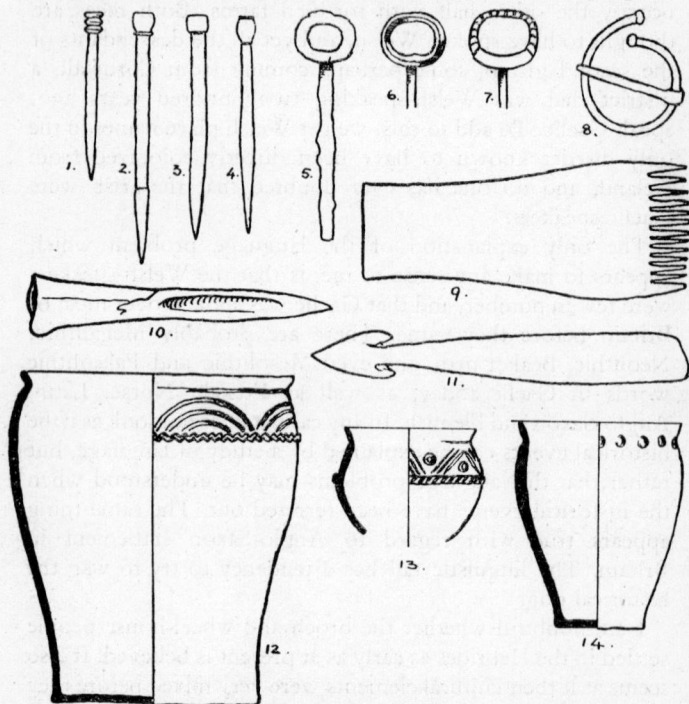

SOME CHARACTERISTIC OBJECTS OF THE BROCH—WHEEL-HOUSE PEOPLE

1—4. Bone pins probably derived from Romano-British types (Daliburgh, South Uist).

5. Iron 'Hand-pin'. A type common at Traprain Law 1st to 4th century A.D. (Daliburgh, South Uist).

6 & 7. Bronze pins from brochs in Caithness. Pins of form 6 were found in a wheel-house in North Uist; in a midden at Gallanach, Oban; in Dun Add and at Traprain Law.

8. Bronze penannular brooch from Skerinish, Skye. Brooches of this type have been found on early Roman camp sites in Scotland.

Continued foot of next page

If you walk along the edge of the great beaches on the west of the Outer Hebrides, where the settlements of the broch people are weathered out of what was once the surface of the fertile machair plain, it is easy to slip back into the Iron Age. Here and there on rocky knobs are little clachans of a few thatched and low-roofed houses, with peat smoke curling from them. Old women and children wander after one or two cows and knit as they go. Tiny fields of oats or rye stand without apparent order here and there. Great heaps of empty shells lie beside the doors of the houses. Greylag geese feed unapproachably in the distant bog. Gannets sweep by above the ocean swells. There is no sense of time and no need to do anything. You are on the rim of the world, and do not seem to have left anything of much importance behind on the other side of the Minch. Even in winter it is much milder than in eastern England. The broch men may well have been very happy there after their long travels. The corn would not grow very well, but their sheep and cattle could find enough to eat. There were deer on the hill, and fish in the sea. Stranded whales could be counted on to eke out the fish oil for the lamps. Fat young seals could be clubbed on the outlying islets and their meat dried for later use. There was still enough wood

---

9. Bone comb, probably for carding wool. This type is common all over Britain from about 300 B.C. onwards. It is of little use for dating.

10. Pointed bone tool possibly used for ornamenting pottery (after Beveridge). This specimen is from Foshigarry, North Uist. Similar bone tools, often described as 'spear-heads' but often found broken by hard usage, are characteristic of the Early Iron Age in southern Britain. They are probably of little value for dating purposes.

11. Bone leaster barb from Foshigarry, North Uist (after Beveridge).

12—14. Reconstructed pot forms. Since the pottery is of a very poor paste no complete pots have as yet been recovered. 13 and 14 are from Daliburgh, South Uist and their shapes are comparatively accurate. 12 is deduced from many small fragments.

(*All small objects to the same scale, No. 1 being* 1¾ *inches long. All pots are also to one scale, No. 12 being* 14 *inches high*).

for what little smelting was necessary. How could people living like that have bothered to go ranting round the seas, or take the art of La Tène into Ireland? They would not do this until the pressure of an increasing population, or a violent climatic change, forced them to go out to fill their empty bellies. Such ills were to come to the Hebrideans, but probably not for many generations. This pretty picture may be absolutely incorrect. The broch people are just as likely to have been an irritable and disgruntled folk, nursing for generation after generation the grievance of the dispossessed. They may never have been quite sure, too, whether a sudden rising of the former owners of the land would not leave them lying with cut throats amid the smoking ruins of their farmsteads. The second picture is probably nearer to the truth than the first. Grandmothers, remembering the miseries of the northward migration, were probably for ever egging on the young men to go out and avenge their misfortunes on some more lucky people.[4]

CHAPTER FOUR

ROMAN INTERLUDE

THE ROMAN INVASION of Scotland was something entirely new in the history of the north. It is usually spoken of as an attempt that failed. Military campaigns had been taking place in southern Britain, partly for the actual aggrandizement of the Imperial power, but partly for strategic reasons. It was intolerable for a respectably-minded and bureaucratic empire to be continually disturbed by barbarian warriors on its northern borders. Julius Cæsar had crushed this trouble in Gaul. It had to be done in Britain.

When we look at Agricola's campaign and the siting of the wall of Pius from the Forth to the Clyde, it is evident that the wars of the north were directed almost entirely against the descendants of the Gallic people, who had built the large stone forts perhaps three hundred years before the days of Agricola. It is hard to believe that, provided, as it obviously was, with an efficient naval force, the Roman higher command could not have organized the destruction of all the brochs and most of their inhabitants. It clearly did not attempt to do so; if it had, it is scarcely credible that the destruction of their towers would have escaped mention in Tacitus' account of his father-in-law Agricola's exploits. The answer surely is that the broch people were hostile to the murus-gallicus tribes, and were either bought off by the Romans, or actively assisted them. When the fleet circumnavigated Scotland, it was probably not on an aggressive expedition against the broch people, but was chasing fugitive elements from the east of Scotland and was hunting out their bases. Nobody could have sited the wall of Pius as they did if sea-borne attacks were expected from the Western Islands.

I think myself that the relatively numerous finds of early

Roman coins made in the Orkneys probably indicate not-infrequent visits by Romano-British merchants, rather than the temporary appearance of a Roman squadron in those waters.

Precisely the same situation seems to have arisen in southern Britain at an earlier date. There are no accounts of prolonged sea and land operations against the Cornovii, or against the Dumnonii and Coritanii of the Midlands. All these people were probably hostile to the more recent Belgic invaders and could easily be bought off or placated. Risings of tribes, like the Iceni, formerly hostile to the Belgæ, were apparently entirely due to Roman mismanagement. The same cause perhaps led the broch people in the end to join hands with the remnants of their former enemies. The condescending attitude of Roman officials may well have had more to do with it than any 'unfortunate incidents' caused by the Roman fleet.

This view is quite unorthodox, and may be proved wrong at any time by the discovery of numerous Agricolan military camps on the west coast to the north of the Mull of Kintyre. I should in any case, however, expect small camps of this period to be found in areas where the murus-gallicus people had formerly established themselves. In particular, there should be one in the coastal district between Mull and the Isle of Skye, another in Lorne, and one on Arran, Bute or Kintyre itself. The Gallic element in these three districts must have been too big to be destroyed by a small force of marines, without the landing of a field force as well. Perhaps this task, through some strategic error, was never undertaken, or could be delegated to the broch people themselves. The whole campaign was never completed; but somebody destroyed the Gallic forts in the west at some unknown date.

There are two problems here to be solved. The first is to try to locate, or establish the absence of, early Roman camps in the west and extreme north of Scotland; their complete absence would indicate that the broch people were at any rate friendly to the Roman invaders. The second is to establish the date at which the murus-gallicus forts were burnt and vitrified. A most necessary work for the understanding of Scottish history is the excavation of the broch of Tirefour on Lismore, in Lorne. This is a key point. It is a broch outpost in a murus-gallicus area. If it was built for defence, and not as a farm, it was intended to control the land route up the Great Glen and the sea route round the coast through the Sound of Mull. This broch should be excavated with the greatest care by highly competent workers. Every scrap of evidence should be saved. The date at which it was built and the manner of its end are of vital historical importance. Was it stormed by furious Welsh tribesmen, or battered down by Roman marines, protected by a testudo of shields? Was it starved out by Dalriadic Scots, or did it survive, peaceful and unharmed,

↑

THE BROCH OF TIRREFOUR ON LISMORE

With the Loch Corrie hills behind and the old sailing coaster Anna Bhan *in front. The broch stands above the old sea cliffs of the 25 foot raised Beach.*

to witness St. Columba rowing by in his curragh on his way
to convert Brude, King of the Picts, at Inverness?

Lismore, the great garden, with its raised beaches and
fuchsias growing by the cottage doors, has seen as much of
history as any place could wish. Round its shores the Mesolithic men have paddled their canoes. Past its rocks the
Megalithic men have travelled. Under the shadow of the
Ardgour hills, gazing across to the distant blue haunch of
Cruachan, the Irish Bronze Age merchants have glided by, on
their way to Denmark. Welshman and Roman must have seen
it. From the walls of Tirefour, men may have watched the
smoke of Dunollie burning at the hands of Saxon spearmen.
Dalriadic Irishmen and saints from Iona, Viking pirates and
Medieval clansmen, all have a say in its story. Last, but
perhaps not least, the great Atlantic convoys have rested in its
shelter. Black-cross bombers have screamed above it; dough-
boys have wandered chewing on its beaches. It is a long, low,
whaleback of an island, insignificant except as a foreground to
the far blue peaks, but it is one of the focal points of British
archaeology.

The tide of Roman occupation ebbed from Scotland, and
the frontier of the provinces of Britain was established at
Hadrian's Wall, with a screen of spies, or scouts, spread out
in front of it. This is often regarded as a defeat for Roman
arms, and it may be so. It may be, however, that Scotland was
regarded, in financial circles, as too poor a country to be
occupied at great expense of men and materials, and that it
was quiet enough to be left for a time to its own devices. How
often have the modern British abandoned a province because
it was turbulent and not worth the cost of keeping under
control? If we could look behind the scenes, I am pretty
certain we should find that some treasury official was responsible for the departure of the eagles from the land of the Picts,
either by cutting down the available garrisons or by removing
them altogether.

It is not clear what started the next series of troubles

between the Roman Empire and the unconquered men of the
north. Apparently there was serious war in the region of
Hadrian's Wall, the date of which is variously placed between
180 A.D. and 205 A.D. The trouble, however, does not appear
to have been of long duration. Between this, however, and the
next Pict war a century later, a new factor enters into the
history of Britain. Saxon pirates appear on the scene. It is
thought that Maximian's admiral Carausius inflicted a serious
reverse on them about 285 A.D. Carausius went on, however,
to set himself up in Britain as a rival Emperor. There were
thus three Emperors: Diocletian the true Emperor; Maximian
his associate, and Carausius a rival or rebel Emperor. Carausius kept his position as Emperor of Britain, striking his
own coinage in London and running his own state, till he was
murdered by Allectus in 294 A.D. Allectus was defeated and
killed by Constantius Chlorus, Maximian's associate in Gaul,
in 296 A.D. This period of rebellion and civil war is important
here only because of a remarkable discovery which has
recently been made in Iceland. In a book called *Gengith Á
Rekja* by Kristjan Eldjarn, the author describes the recovery
of three Roman coins from the head of Hamarsfjord, in
south-east Iceland. These coins had apparently weathered out
from old habitation sites and were found lying on the debris
from these sites at different places at the head of the fjord. The
coins are all *antoniniani* and were struck by Aurelian, Probus
and Diocletian. The date of their loss could have been about
300 A.D. Eldjarn is convinced that these coins were not
brought by Vikings to Iceland, or carried there in recent
years. He thinks that some ship from Carausius fleet may have
been driven to Iceland by stress of weather, while rounding
up Saxon pirates. In any case the find appears to indicate that
people from the Roman world reached Iceland about six
hundred years after the days of Pytheas.

Now the distribution of Roman coins of this period, outside
the Roman provinces in Britain, is curious. There are two
finds from Galway in Western Ireland; one in central Ireland;

one on Islay; one on Uist; and a find, made in the eighteenth century, of numerous coins of Diocletian in a pot near Fort Augustus on Loch Ness. Many of the coins from Scotland and Ireland were minted in Alexandria. Carausius had his own mint in London and his coins are very common in southern Britain, but I can find no other record of one north of the Walls. Diocletian was famous for his persecution of Christians.

If Carausius' ships reached Iceland, it must have been before he opened his own mint. He would never bother to pay his navy with coins imported from abroad, when his own were easily obtained, unless there was a large accumulated stock of the former in Britain. If there was such a stock, the opening of a mint appears to be unnecessary.

The distribution of *antoniniani*, as these coins are called, in Scotland and Ireland is peculiar in itself, for coins of the third century are otherwise unknown in the Scottish Highlands, and practically so in Ireland. It looks as if, during the reign of Diocletian, people were flying beyond the Empire for security. Even more peculiar than this is the location of Hamarsfjord for the discovery of *antoniniani* in Iceland, for, of the three places mentioned in the *Landnamabok* as being former habitations of Irish monks, two, Papyle and Papos, are within a few miles distance. Papyle is, in fact, some ten miles out to sea at the mouth of the fjord. Is it possible that these three Icelandic coins are an indication that Christians were already beginning to seek out 'desert' places for meditation as early as the days of Diocletian's persecution? If they were, did they know that Thule was there ready for them? It seems most probable that they did.

This is the only gleam of light to come through the dark curtain of ignorance from the days of Pytheas till those of St. Columba, but it is enough to show that many facts, as yet unguessed, are there for the seeking. It does not necessarily mean more than a chance visit to Iceland and, if the visitors were shipwrecked seamen, they are unlikely to have survived the winter. I think, however, that it means more than this.

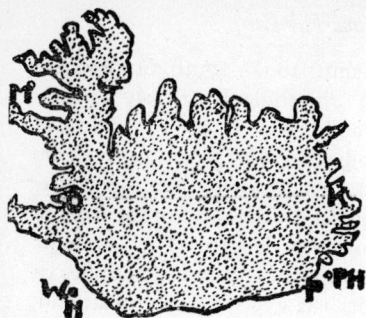

THE SETTLEMENTS OF THE
CELTIC MONKS IN THE
NORTHERN SEAS

W.=Norse place name containing
   'Westmann' meaning Celt.

P.=Name compounded from Norse
   'Papar' meaning Priests.

H.=Hermitage. Known or inferred.

K.=Norse name containing word for
   church.

M.=Monasteries of Iona and Flatey.

O.=Orlyg's settlement.

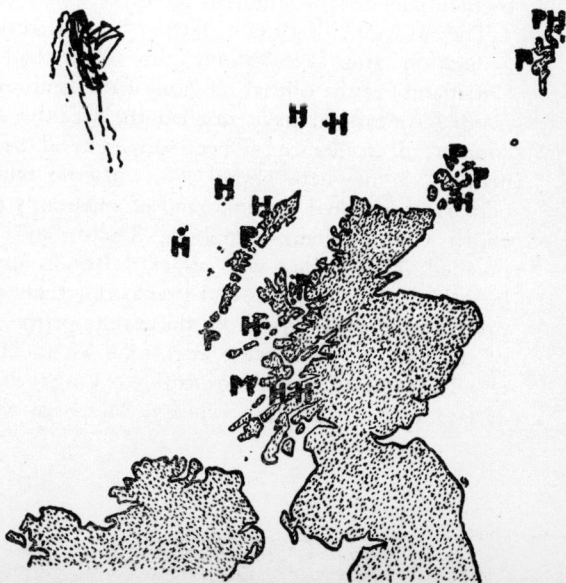

The centre of interest now shifts to the south. Somewhere between 300 A.D. and 400 A.D., the students of early climatic changes have observed a new and intense return of a cold and wet period. This is based, as before, on the dates given by archaeologists to their finds. This clearly intensified the pressure of barbarian tribes against the defences of the Roman Empire all along their enormous length. The strategic problems of the defence were impossible to meet; supplies of fighting men were too limited; distances were too great; and, above all, the cost was too high. Looking at the situation now, and comparing it with wars of modern times, it appears that the Roman army put up a wonderful resistance. Again and again tribes broke through the defensive cordons, ravaged great territories, doing untold damage, and were then brought to a stand. Had there been any co-ordination between the attackers, the Empire must have collapsed centuries before it did. It survived, however, long enough to spread the germs of civilization among all its enemies. Gaul certainly suffered worse than Britain. Its trials began a century earlier and it was completely conquered. Large areas in the west of Britain considered themselves as Roman, and were spoken of as such by their enemies for hundreds of years.

The invasions of Britain did not become really bad for a generation after Constantine the Great had proclaimed Christianity as the official religion of the Empire. No serious trouble appears to have reached the wealthy south of the country, till an alliance had been formed by all the surrounding peoples. Somewhere about 366 A.D., the whole mass of barbarians attacked in some kind of apparently synchronized effort: Gaul, Britain, Pannonia, Thrace and Africa were invaded. The peoples who attacked Britain appear to have been Irish, Picts, Saxons and Franks. Of these the Picts had probably suffered most from the results of the deterioration of the climate. They were after food as much as anything else. The cattle raid was an institution among the Celtic peoples as late as the eighteenth century. The Irish were probably out for the excitement, loot and slaves, while it has been suggested that the Saxons wanted loot to buy off the peoples who were pressing on them from the east. Somewhere about 367 A.D. the defence of Britain collapsed: the fleet was at least partly destroyed and the army scattered. The situation was restored under Count Theodosius, with the help of troops from Gaul, a year or two later, but many captives, many fat bullocks and much loot left the country never to return. The process was repeated at uncertain dates down to about 450 A.D. The last mentioned defeat of the Picts by the Britons is in about the year 429 A.D. This may have taken place in Scotland, for one result of the troubles appears to have been the re-establishment of a Roman province north of the Wall of Hadrian. Roman squadrons, under Theodosius' orders, appear once more in the Orkneys slaughtering Picts. Thule is mentioned, but it is not at all sure what Thule meant in this connexion. Probably it meant the Shetlands, but Lewis is a possibility.

Fourth-century Roman coins have been found all up the east of Scotland. They may have been looted, but they may indicate the presence of troops in Roman pay. There seems to be little doubt that Roman officers organized local troops to defend their own homes against attacks from further north, or against Saxons from the east. These troops were to form the nucleus of the British Kingdom of Strathclyde in years to come. Some part of them, drawn apparently from Ptolemy's Otadinoi, living between the Forth and the Tweed, were moved bodily into North Wales to drive out Irish settlers there. They succeeded in this task and their descendants became the famous spearmen of Powis. This is a very confused and difficult period to study. As far as one can judge the whole balance in Scotland had changed. The south had become a Roman province and was soon to become a British or Welsh kingdom; the Murus Gallicus and broch men had combined for war and had become generally known as Picts. Somewhere between the middle of the fifth and the beginning of the sixth

century, Irishmen came over in bulk and settled the Dalriadic
Kingdom, now known as Argyll. These are the first Scots
named in Scotland; before this all Scots were Irishmen. There
is no indication in history whether this settlement was effected
by force of arms or not.

One of the great difficulties in early history is the widespread
habit of calling peoples by the names of their ruling families.
Not all the Burgundians, who occupied Southern Gaul, can
have come from the small island of Bornholm, in the Baltic,
not all the Goths from Gotland. In the same way, the small
settlement of Scots in Argyll cannot have superseded the mass
of inhabitants already in Scotland. They did, however,
conquer a small part of Pictland and give the country a ruling
family. In this manner Megalithic, Beaker and Urn folk,
Gauls, Saxons, Normans and Irishmen have all become Scots,
that is Irishmen. People on the Continent today think of the
whole of Britain as England and the whole population as
Englishmen. 'Perfidious Albion' has shrunk to the small
Highland area of Breadalbane.

Let us go back to the captives hurried over the Irish Sea to
the original land of the Scots. A famous raiding high king,
Nial of the Nine Hostages, appears to have organized the
whole of Ireland for this purpose. He met his end, appro-
priately enough for our story, on the Muir-nan-Icht—the sea
of the Ictis of Pytheas. Some believe the *Chronicle's* story that
he was killed in 405 A.D., but others, including Chadwick,
place it thirty years or more later. At any rate, tradition holds
him responsible for carrying off among his numerous captives
the Patron Saint of Ireland. Patrick, an educated man, though
he speaks of his learning with contempt, was only one of
hundreds carried into slavery. Although something of a
disaster to themselves, their captivity was the cause of an Irish
Renascence.[5]

Even if all records had been destroyed, archaeologists
would have been able to deduce that some great trouble had
occurred towards the beginning of the fifth century after

Christ. In East Anglia in particular, but scattered also over the whole of southern Britain, finds have been made which show that men buried their treasures in haste and never returned to dig them up again. The great silver find, now known as the Mildenhall Treasure although it was made at West Row, is only a particularly spectacular example of many. In the immediate neighbourhood of Mildenhall alone, I have records of the discovery of eight hoards. If the area is extended a few miles into the Fenland and along the Icknield Way belt, the number rises to twenty. Many of these hoards consist of pewter table-vessels, others of pots full of late Roman silver, including coins of Honorius. One of several finds near Icklingham, in Suffolk, consisted of silver coins, brooches, rings and a spoon, together with gold beads and ingots. It seems that these objects are all later than the great disaster of 367 A.D., but they may well belong to the time of the raids of Nial of the Nine Hostages. The coin hoards normally go down to the reign of Honorius and represent the last Imperial money to reach Britain in any quantity, for the Gallic mints were destroyed by barbarian invasions about 406 A.D. The concealment of these treasures need not, therefore, have taken place so early as it might appear. An entry in the *Anglo-Saxon Chronicle*, under the year 418 A.D., is interesting in this connexion, for it states that in this year the Romans collected all the treasures that were in Britain; some they hid in the earth so that no man has been able to find them and some they took with them into Gaul. This has much the appearance of being the result of a Government instruction to check Saxon raids by removing the source of temptation. The fact that it is mentioned in the Chronicle reflects the disappointment it caused to the raiders. Incidentally, it shows how unreliable is the date 410 A.D., which was once firmly believed to be that of the departure of all Romans from Britain. In fact they never did depart. The British inhabitants were Romans in their own eyes and as far as their status as citizens went.

Almost more interesting than these hoards buried in

England are the traces which are found from time of the raiders at home. Silver treasures have been found in two places in Ireland (Coleraine and Balline), and at Traprain Law in Scotland. In all these treasures, beautiful late-Roman silver vessels have been hacked into pieces ready to be shared out by weight to the members of the robber force. We have actual written accounts of this being done in Gaul. The two Irish treasures were probably deposited by much the same band that carried off St. Patrick, the Traprain Treasure by Picts or Saxons.

It is interesting to observe that, in a find of pewter vessels made in the bed of the old Croft River, at Welney in the Fens, this same practice had been in process of being carried out. Two complete vessels were found during the war, and, when we came to investigate the site recently, we found a small dish in the river bed sliced in two with shears and doubled up. It is clear what had happened. Raiders had been sacking the Romano-British buildings which had stood on the river bank. They had found the pewter, which they thought to be silver, and were cutting it up to be shared out, when someone came along who recognized the character of the metal. 'You are not going to carry that heavy old stuff home with you?' he asked. Whereupon they threw it all in the river in disgust.

These late-Roman hoards known to date from a period of great disturbance remind us of the Bronze Age hoards found in so many places in England, and also in Scotland. These mostly belong to the late part of the Bronze Age and contain numerous objects broken in pieces, hammered flat, or melted into metal cakes, which are seldom complete. Generally, if a sword or spear has been broken up, only a piece or two of it is found in a particular hoard. They are spoken of as 'founders' hoards' and are thought to represent stocks belonging to itinerant bronze workers, who hid them and then got into trouble. This is clearly not the case. Of the three hoards of this type of which I have had personal experience, two were buried in little holes in the ground at no great distance from one another, while the third was being carried in a wooden keg over a causeway in the Fens when it fell off and was lost in the bog. It looks very much as if we have here again evidence of war booty shared up in the same way as the silver of later times. If this is so, it indicates very widespread trouble at the end of the Bronze Age and probably reflects the invasions of the earliest Celtic tribes. The reason why it so often remained in the ground may well be that, with the coming of cheap iron, it lost its value. I regard any attempts at dating based on the association of objects as quite unreliable. Men may have kept their war booty for years in holes under the floors of their huts, adding an old axe or broken spear from time to time, while waiting for the bronze merchant to come and collect it. In many cases he never came: the metal had become almost valueless.

We have seen the arrival of hundreds and perhaps thousands of Romano-British slaves in Ireland. No doubt many were dragged off into Scotland also. Many, if not most, of these captives were Christians. The religion of their captors is unknown, but is spoken of as Druidical. The Irish are a kindly people. It is most unlikely that the servitude of these British captives was anything like so unpleasant as the experiences of central Europeans who were taken from their homes to forced labour in Russia. Those I have talked to who had this misfortune clearly went through trials which no horse would ever experience in Ireland at any period of history. Moreover, these captives in Ireland had messages to give to their captors which would soon take the fancy of an imaginative people. They had new forms of ornament, new ways of doing things, news of unknown countries, but above all a new religion. To a dreamy people, who had only to step out of their doors to see the mist swirling on the hill, or the sun shining on the surface of the loch, this religion had an instant appeal. It was a message that took their fancy, in the same way as their ancient stories of heroes and adventure appealed to them. 'There were giants in those days', they always tell you. Here was another giant of a different kind. They had always believed in the transmigration of souls. Here was a religion which explained what really happened to their souls. It was so much more sensible than worshipping a rowan tree, that we can hardly be surprised at the speed of their conversion. 'St. Patrick was a gentleman and came of decent people'. He could talk to anybody in a way they could understand, even if he put Ps into his words where they used Qs. It only needed a man with fiery enthusiasm to sway the whole people to his way of thinking. A great leader is so often of a slightly different race from the people he leads; no one has known him as a sticky-fingered little boy.

CHAPTER FIVE

SAXON, SCOT AND PICT

THE MATERIAL EVIDENCE of trade between Roman Britain and
Ireland is very slight. There are a few coins and a few brooches
mostly of an early date. When, however, we come to the end of
the period, it is evident that the British captives were having
an influence on their masters. Professor Sean O'Riordain has
brought this altogether in a most important recent paper
printed in the *Proceedings of the Royal Irish Academy*. He points
to pottery of sub-Roman type being made in Ireland, and he
also shows that bronze vessels like skillets, and also small
toilet implements, were being made of a sub-Roman form.
A civilizing, as well as a missionary movement, was in
progress.

When we turn to Scotland it is not so easy to trace a similar
process, but this may only be because no one has gone deeply
into the matter. People clearly moved between Scotland and
England on peaceful errands in Roman times. Bronze pins of
second- to fourth-century date are found from time to time.
There were two at the Lydney temple in Gloucestershire, one
at Sandy in Bedfordshire, and one at Newnham in Cambridge.
Doubtless there are others. The Romano Britons, however,
did not apparently trade their brooches to the broch people.
Merchants sometimes reached the Hebrides. Roman pottery
has been found on Tiree and in the Outer Islands. A votive, or
token, wool bale was found in a broch in Skye. The com-
parative dearth of objects does not appear to indicate a lack of
commerce; it may only indicate a lack of interest in durable
objects. Fine raiment may have been more popular than
brooches or kettles. Brooches spread to some extent in the
east of Scotland, but as yet only early types have been recognized. Even more striking than this lack of Roman evidence

if that of evidence of Anglo-Saxon settlement. Many writers have assumed a very early occupation of the shores of the Forth by Frisian or Saxon immigrants. There is not the slightest trace of this. The only objects of Anglo-Saxon manufacture that I have been able to trace in this area are the well-known beads from the stone cist grave at Dalmeny. The biconical form of several of these beads is such as is only found in very late pagan or Christian burials in England, and I do not think that they can be earlier than the end of the sixth century A.D. Beads of the same type were found in the broch, dun Fiardhart in Skye, which produced the token wool bale.

Further evidence that Anglo-Saxon objects were reaching the west of Scotland in the seventh and eighth centuries, is the 'elastic' wire ring found at Baleshare in North Uist and figured in Erskine Beveridge's book on the island. But where are the traces of the early settlers in the east? A pot, which might be from a Frisian 'Angle' source, may have been found at Buchan in Aberdeenshire, but part of its label is known to be incorrect. In any case one Anglian cremation does not make a settlement. Who is wrong? Where are all the graves of the Bernician settlers? Were there ever more than a few Saxon settlers in Northumberland and Scotland, who formed a small military caste and then organized the descendants of the British tribes as a Saxon kingdom? In connexion with this name of Bernicia, was there any reason to doubt Ridgeway's suggestion that it was a scribe's error for Berwicia, comparable to the mistakes which turned Iowa into Iona and Aebudes into Hebrides? Why do the people of Berwick still speak of 'the Kingdoms of England and Scotland *and* the town of Berwick-upon-Tweed'?

I do not know the answer to any of these questions, but the very fact that I can ask them shows how much we have to learn. The tramping armies of Ecgfrith, smashed by Brude III, King of the Picts, in 685 A.D. at Dunnichen in Angus, may have been almost entirely composed of Celtic men. I find it hard to believe in an extensive early Saxon settlement in Scotland unaccompanied by the slightest trace of the well-known pagan burial rites. It just does not make sense. Neither could all the building, road-making, quarrying, and so on, have gone on in Scotland for years, without finding one of their cemeteries if they were at all numerous. Nor do I believe that Saxon settlers changed their burial rites the moment they stepped ashore. Something is very wrong here. I think it must be the interpretation put by historians upon the ancient documents. It seems to be a case parallel to the change in name of the Picts into Scots. The name of the ruling caste has been applied to their people. I believe this habit to be one of the greatest obstacles to the interpretation of early history.

Two or three spears, which may have been of Anglo-Saxon manufacture, were found during the excavations at Traprain Law. Since both Pict and Saxon were ravaging Britain together, there is no need to be surprised at this. They may even have been taken from Saxon enemies during the traditional wars of Arthur.

Unless I am much mistaken, however, the Anglo-Saxons did leave a lasting impression on the Highlanders. Their round brooches were copied and used right through the medieval period until the present day. The Frankish purse, adopted by the Saxons in the seventh century, became the well-known sporran. More important, perhaps, the teutonic dirk or scramasax, used by their warriors from Sweden to the shores of Italy, was adopted by the Saxons in the seventh century. This weapon must frequently have been seen during the wars of that time in Scotland. The Highlanders took it over, and you can still see it swinging beside their kilted legs.

From a ship at sea off the Mull of Kintyre, the Irish coast is plainly visible. It can be a wild and stormy sea enough, for the great North Atlantic swell rolls right up it, but I have seen it like a mirror with basking sharks leaping from its silvered surface. It is no wonder that it has never been a barrier between Scotland and Ireland. As far back in time as we can trace human habitation in western Scotland, we can see that people were passing between there and Ireland, sometimes as friends

G

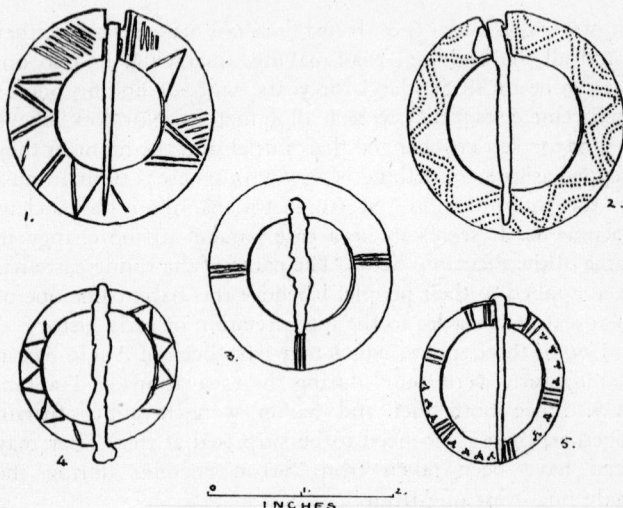

BRONZE 'PLAID' BROOCHES

(A problem for Typologists)

1.　　　From the plaid of an old woman in South Uist in 1870 A.D.
2.　　　From North Uist (after Beveridge).
3—5.　　From Pagan Anglo-Saxon graves at Holywell Row, Suffolk, 6th.
　　　　to 7th century A.D.

This form of brooch persisted right through the Middle Ages. The Saxons apparently learnt its use in Southern Britain after their settlement in the country. Both groups of brooches shown here are chosen at random from many possible examples. It is probable that they are degenerate copies of more elaborate examples in valuable metals, but even if this is so the general form appears to have persisted for hundreds of years. The resemblance even includes two different methods of construction. 1, 3 and 4 are cut from sheet metal, 2 and 5 are formed from overlapping strips.

Martin, writing in 1716 A.D., gives an interesting description of the wearing of plaid brooches: 'The ancient dress wore by the women and which is yet wore by some of the vulgar, called Arisad, is a white plaid, having a few small stripes of black, blue, and red. It reached from the neck to the heels, and was tied before on the breast with a buckle of silver or brass, according to the quality of the person. I have seen some of the former of a hundred marks value; it was broad as an ordinary pewter plate, the whole curiously engraved with various animals etc. There was a lesser buckle which was wore in the middle of the larger and above two ounces in weight; it had in the centre a large piece of crystal or some finer stone, and this was set all round with several finer stones of a lesser size.'

and often as foes. Nobody knows whether the migration of
the Dalriadic Scots from Antrim to Argyll was peaceful or
was the result of war. On the whole, it seems more probable
that it was carried out in peace. Chadwick, who has written at
length upon the matter, considered that it took place more
than fifty years before the generally accepted date at the
beginning of the sixth century. Some of the sons of Erc,
Fergus, Angus and Loarn, who are said to have led the
expedition, stole St. Patrick's horses. Fergus had a grand-
daughter who was blessed by the saint. The accepted date of
St. Patrick's death is about 461 A.D. Archaeology can at
present say nothing either for or against this suggestion.
Absolutely nothing has been done which could help us to
clear up the problem, except the excavation of Dun Add near
the Crinan canal. Dun Add is thought to have been the seat
of Gabran, son of Fergus. It should have been occupied about
500 A.D. The excavation of this hill fort was not recorded as
an excavation would have been today, and it is hard to
separate the objects which were found at different levels.
There is, however, among them one ring-headed bronze pin,
which is of a type common at Traprain Law in the first and
second centuries A.D. Specimens of this type of pin, cast from
a mould, have been also found in the broch of Ness in
Caithness and in a midden at Gallanach near Oban. Others
have been found in various places.

This scrap of evidence is too small to be of much importance, but it should be kept in mind in case other facts emerge
in future to suggest that the Dalriadic settlement was much
earlier than is at present thought. The shapes of ring-headed
pins go through a remarkable series of changes and ought to
be as valuable for dating purposes as any type of personal
object. The discovery of this particular specimen may only,
however, indicate that Dun Add was occupied long before the
days of Fergus or Gabran. In which case the other objects
from the fort, which appear to date from the sixth to the
eighth centuries, will give a better picture. I have never heard

of any objects of this period being found at Dunollie, the
reputed seat of Fergus' brother Loarn. I am not even clear in
my own mind as to whether Loarn ever existed, or whether
the whole story has been made up to explain, among other
things, the name of the district. This was apparently known
to Ptolemy as 'Longus', or some word resembling it, and is
now known as Lorne. All we really know is that the Scots
were firmly settled in Argyll in the days of St. Columba, who,
we are told, converted the northern Picts near Inverness about
565 A.D. Irishmen went hunting on Arran, according to their
Heroic Stories, hundreds of years before this. They may well
have been continually passing backwards and forwards for a
thousand years before St. Columba, or even two thousand.
The process continued until the days of the Georges. My own
relations are said to have crossed to Ulster more than once,
when Lochaber got too hot for them.

We cannot, I think, separate the stories of Western Scotland
and Northern Ireland. They are all mixed together. We can,
however, work away at the archaeology until we get our
dating of objects straightened out. Then, and not before, it
may be possible to distinguish new arrivals from the old.
Chadwick, for instance, is inclined to see in the story of
Labraid Loingseach, the seaman who, if Ridgeway is right,
first brought iron weapons from Gaul into Ireland and is said
to have smitten eight towers in Tiree, evidence that expeditions
were undertaken long before the fifth century A.D. against the
broch men or, as he thinks, the Fomorians. This may be true,
but why not excavate some of the towers on Tiree and see
what story they tell? There are certainly four or more circular
structures on Tiree, but Beveridge, in his *Coll and Tiree*, does
not think that they were ever tall towers. I have not seen them
myself. I should like to think of Loingseach striding up the
sands of Gott Bay in an embossed bronze jockey-cap helmet,
and wearing a long La Tène sword in a sheath ornamented
with cunning Celtic spirals. It is easy to picture the background, with the distant hills of Mull and Ardnamurchan

reflected in blue water and the peculiar shapes of the Treshnish Islands. But did it ever happen at all?

If Sir Lindsay Scott is right, the men living in those round Tiree buildings were peaceful farmers with precious little to reward Loingseach's men for their trouble and danger. At best Loingseach was rooting out a nest of pirate-farmers; at worst he was nothing more than his name implies—a seaman and freebooter. But in Ireland he was a legendary hero and his deeds were sung for hundreds of years. How much distortion crept in with the telling of them? How many new places were added to the story? There is absolutely no way of finding out. In the comparable stories of Saxo Grammaticus from Denmark, we find Norse characters introduced from places like Iceland, which they had not apparently even visited in the days of the heroes whose exploits were sung. All this crept in many years later. 'He was a great man, a great hero, a giant, he would have been a great sailor, with a name like that to him. He would be going to Tiree surely, and Skye and the Orkneys itself, so he would'. But is there a single word of truth in it? There is truth in the general idea, but there may be none at all in the details.

It is just the same with Loarn, Fergus, Angus and Gabran. 'If they had come from Ireland, they would surely have met St. Patrick if they were anybody at all. Indeed it would be so'. But they may have been dead two hundred years already! Let us not be so damnably cautious. We will believe in the whole lot of them, and in Finn, and the grand old man Cæilte, who shocked St. Patrick with his amorous stories, although he had been dead two hundred years. They are strong and vivid and romantic, and worth more than the dating of five hundred stone forts, with two thousand tons of potsherds and a bucket full of bronze pins. What does it matter if the dates are wrong and the names are all invented? Men lived like that in the Celtic Iron Age, with their feuds, their cattle and their horses. They sailed, they fished and they hunted, they courted and they quarrelled and they had far more joyous lives than anyone making ten thousand a year in an office. I should like to have seen someone trying to peddle 'social security' to one of Finn's spearmen. But there are still things in the world which they would appreciate. The circling cloud of Spitfires roaring from an airfield into the blue sky in the Battle of Britain; the shot-torn Fortress bombers struggling home through a snowstorm; the destroyer washing down in a south-west gale and the infantry following up behind the armour. These would have made them shout with appreciation and delight.

Southern Scotland is believed to have been a Christian land long before the north. Much doubt exists as to the precise date of the foundation of St. Ninian's mission church at Whithorn in Galloway, but it may have been founded by the middle of the fifth century. Coroticus, a chief or King of the Strathclyde area whose soldiers and seamen raided Ireland in the time of St. Patrick, was apparently a Christian. The northern Picts were still heathens and had druids. St. Columba was an Irish noble and was descended, it is said, from Nial of the Nine Hostages himself. He was given Iona for his central church by the Dalriadic chiefs, with whom he was apparently on terms of ancient friendship. His missionary work does not seem to have met with so much opposition as that of Patrick in Ireland. Only in the Orkneys were his companions ever in personal danger. We need not think that all the men of Scotland became even nominal Christians immediately. Traces of druidism, or nature-worship, survived in Scotland for more than a thousand years. They may still exist, but Scotland was soon a Christian land. With its acceptance, churches and monastic settlements sprang up all over the country. Very soon groups of monks began to found their curious settlements on lonely islands. This passion for seeking 'deserts' for contemplation goes back to the time of St. Columba at the latest. In the lands around the Mediterranean, it was in full swing in the days before St. Patrick's mission. In Egypt it may be older still.

The most interesting account of an attempt to find such a

desert is described in Adamnan's life of St. Columba. It is probably the most remarkable glimpse of geographical adventure since the days of Pytheas, and must have taken place about 600 A.D. Four hundred years or so before the days of Eric the Red, Cormac, we are told, set out in search of a desert. For fourteen days he was carried northward by a southerly gale. Then, as a result, it seemed, of prayer, the wind changed and he came back again. This in itself is no more than a garbled account of what happened. A detail, however, is preserved, which makes it clear that Cormac, or somebody Adamnan knew about, had reached a country which we can recognize. I do not know whether anyone has noticed this before and I am sure I should not have done so had I not been there myself. In the far north, so the story goes, Cormac's vessel was attacked by myriads of loathsome stinging creatures about the size of frogs, which almost pierced the sides of the boat. The exaggeration is typically Irish, or may have meant the tiny frogs which are sometimes sucked out of a pond by a williwaw and dropped all over the ground somewhere else. To anyone who has seen them, the myriads of loathsome stinging creatures are obvious. It is an almost perfect description of the Greenland mosquitoes. These are such a nuisance in summer that they could reasonably be compared to a plague of Egypt. They are so numerous and so voracious that no one who has met them will ever forget the experience. The thickest cloud of Highland midges is nothing, the flies of Iceland not worth remarking. The mosquitoes of Greenland are a veritable cloud of loathsome stinging creatures. They would not bite through the leather sides of a curragh but they seem as if they could, nor are they as big as frogs, but they seem as if they are. No drifting icebergs, no mountain scenery, no icecaps glittering in the sun mean anything at all when the mosquitoes are at work. I have not the slightest doubt that Cormac, or somebody at that time, reached Greenland. The story may have no connexion with Cormac; the number of days may be incorrect; but the loathsome cloud of stinging creatures is a detail which is as true as Pytheas' frozen sea; somebody must have seen it.

Let us for once indulge in an entirely imaginary picture, and believe that we can see St. Columba walking up the beach on Iona, with his arm round Cormac's shoulder. Behind them a group of anxious monks are gathered about the salt-stained curragh and her bearded crew. A sad sing-song voice is saying, 'as big as frogs, and they could almost bite through the side of the boat itself'.

Very few people in Britain today can have had any first-hand experience in a curragh. Fortunately, some years before his death, James Hornell, the great student of marine archaeology, published a full account of all he could learn about this type of boat, in his *British Coracles and Irish Curraghs*. Since, however, this book is probably not widely read and many people have not the slightest idea what a curragh is like, I feel I ought to say something about them and also about the Greenland umiak. Perhaps I should add that I have been out in a Kerry curragh and have had the opportunity of making a careful examination of a Greenland umiak.

There can, I think, be little doubt that the curragh was evolved from a skin boat, very like those still used in Tibet, but modified by contact with the round coracles of the rivers, and either dug-out canoes or primitive plank-built boats. Practically every boat is a compromise or hybrid resulting from the builder trying to make the best of many ideas. The Tibetan boat is a rectangular frame of four pieces of wood. From two sides of this frame four or more light sticks are bent round in a curve and are fastened to the opposite sides. Over the whole a skin is stretched and is lashed to the four original wooden frames. The result is a trough-shaped skin-covered boat. The curragh was originally of this shape, but at some unknown date two pieces of wood were substituted for the single piece at one end. These two pieces are secured to the longer sides, raked up at an angle, and joined together to form a bow. From this framework numerous light rods are bent round from side to side, and also longitudinal wands, or stringers, are placed at intervals up the sides, making a form of basket. The original five pieces form the gunwale; there is no keel. I have built one of these boats as an experiment. It takes very little time, but uses a great quantity of twine for lashings. The size of a curragh could vary according to the number of skins you wished to employ. As it increased in size, the framework would naturally have to become rather stouter. The curragh of western Ireland today is undoubtedly smaller than some of those used in antiquity. The normal type carries four men with ease, and is often about sixteen foot long.

The Greenland umiak is in some ways more closely related to the shape of the primitive skin boat of Tibet. The gunwale consists of two long poles pulled together at the ends and joined by two short pieces. The rest of the framework is, however, constructed like a plank-built boat. There is an internal keel, floor and side timbers or ribs, stem and stern posts. The whole construction has clearly been much influenced by wooden boats of the Viking type. The umiak has a small square-sail; the early curragh voyagers used a sail; the modern curragh is almost entirely a pulling boat.

In process of time in some districts, notably on the Scottish rivers and the north-west coast of England, the curragh shape became copied in wood, and is now known as a coble. Ceubol was apparently the Welsh name for a curragh. Professor A. Ross traces this name back to a name for skin boats in Mesopotamia. The curragh, the coble and some fishing boats in Portugal are rowed in a manner not observed elsewhere in western Europe. A heavy block of wood, known as a 'bull', is fastened to the loom of the oar and this swivels on a single thole pin in the gunwale of the boat. This was clearly a pre-Roman method of rowing, spread all up the western seaboard of Europe. It may go back to Megalithic times.

The umiak is rowed with the loom of the oar passing through a raw-hide grommet attached to the gunwale.

Umiaks today are, or were in 1937, covered with eight hides taken from bearded seals or walrus. They may run up to twenty six feet or more in length. At one time they have been larger. Irish curraghs were certainly built of this size and sometimes considerably bigger. Some authorities throw doubt on the seventeenth-century picture of a large sea-going curragh, preserved in the Pepysian Library at Cambridge. This is a very large curragh under sail and towing a dug-out canoe. Even if it is not an accurate picture, which it well may be, it certainly depicts the traditional appearance of such a boat. The drawing also illustrates the construction; it is, like the umiak, modelled on the framework of plank-built boats. There is no reason why this should not have been the case.

Many years ago, a hoard of gold objects, including a model boat, was found at Broighter in Ireland. The latest objects in the hoard date from about the birth of Christ. Judging from the number of rowing thwarts, this boat must have been a model of a vessel about fifty feet in length, not unlike that shown on the Pepysian drawing. She was square-rigged, had a steering oar on the port side, and was double-ended. She was rowed with grommets round the oars. Whether this model represents a wooden or hide-covered boat, it shows that relatively large vessels could be seen in Ireland at this time.

The curragh is remarkably light and buoyant. Although rather alarming to those accustomed to the more ponderous movements of a wooden boat, she is probably as safe, or safer, at sea than any undecked boat of her size. The curragh is so light that she can ride over seas which would swamp heavier open boats. Owing to her lightness, she can travel at great speed. There is nothing improbable in a large curragh reaching Iceland from Scotland in six days with favourable winds, or Greenland in fourteen days. The curragh was clearly more popular with the Irish voyagers than contemporary wooden boats. St. Brendan, whose story, though it may be largely mythical, is nevertheless full of information, was persuaded against his will to use a wooden boat for his second long voyage. For the first he used three curraghs each holding twenty men.

The only reason why I doubt the passage of umiaks from America or Greenland to Scotland in the early centuries of our era is the improbability of their crews being accidentally provided with enough to drink on the voyage. Had they been so provided, the umiak could have made the crossing. If men can sail dories across the North Atlantic as they have done, they could sail umiaks.

It is a remarkable picture, this voyaging of Christian monks to the far north. The skin boat skimmed like a stormy petrel over the surface of the ocean. An endless succession of fulmars glided by and peered like owls into the men's faces. The man at the helm held his course by watching the run of the seas and was guided only by the occasional appearance of the sun by day and the stars by night. If, however, he could steer even approximately north, he could not miss Iceland. The hills are too high, and can be seen from miles off the land.

I once asked a Norwegian how he thought his ancestors knew their position at sea. He replied that they picked a louse out of their shirt and it would always turn to the north. This is only another way of saying that they did it by observing nature. The long ocean swells run true and parallel for days at a time. You have only to hold the same angle to them to keep your course. Returning from Jan Mayen to Norway on one occasion, we observed that when a Norwegian seaman, and not one of ourselves, was at the wheel he hardly ever glanced at the compass card. He steered for four hours entirely by the run of the seas. We were not far out in making our landfall.

Then there is the flight of birds. In the summer great masses of puffins, guillemots, gannets and the rest come ashore to breed, but they fly far out to sea to fish for food in the day time. Even when you are a long way out of sight of land, the majestic flight of the homing gannets will show you where the land lies. Of course it is no good watching a non-breeder. One of these followed us half-way across the North Atlantic.

Seas, sun, stars and birds, then, were the guides of the ancient navigators in the north. They were by no means as inefficient as we may think today, with our radar and our echo-sounding. Norse seamen have told me, too, that the latitude was roughly estimated long ago by lying flat in the bottom of the boat and guessing the angle between an out-stretched arm pointed at the sun at its highest and the mast. This method, however, is probably relatively modern.

CHAPTER SIX

THE CELTS IN ICELAND

PEOPLE MAY DOUBT that Cormac reached Greenland, or that Brendan saw the volcanoes of Iceland. They may dismiss the stories of ancient voyages far over the western seas to the 'Land of Women'. It is impossible, however, to doubt the straightforward account in Dicuil's book on the measurement of the earth. Dicuil wrote his book about 825 A.D.; thirty years before that he had talked to a party of monks who had returned from a summer in Thule. It was so light at midnight in summer, they said, that they could see to pick the lice out of their shirts. What a beautiful Irish way of describing the Midnight Sun! It is as easily understood as their standard of measurement, 'as thick as the black of a nail'. Dicuil then vouches for the voyagers. Bede says that the voyages took six days. The Norse *Landnamabok* tells that there were Christian men living in Iceland before the Norse settled there in the ninth century and that their relics were found in Papyle and Papos. 'Their relics were found there; Irish books, bells and croziers and other things besides'. In another book, *Merlin's Island*, I have illustrated bronze *styli* for writing, found in Iceland, which I believe may have been some of these other things.

Various trifling details in the *Landnamabok* make it clear that the Irish and Scottish monks knew far more about Iceland, and that their settlements were more widely distributed, than might have been expected. A translation of the *Landnamabok* was published by the Rev. T. Ellwood in 1908, and the quotations which follow are from this work.

In the first place, after describing the discovery of the bells and books and croziers, there is a remark, 'and it is stated in English books that in those times voyages were made between these countries'. Now this statement is clearly made in addition to the mention of voyages made by Bede in his book *De Ratione Temporum*, which must have been written before Bede's death in 735 A.D., which is in itself ninety years before Dicuil's work on the measurement of the earth. There must have been in existence at the time the *Landnamabok* was compiled by Ari the Learned, who died in 1148 A.D., quite a number of books which described early expeditions to Iceland. It is possible that centres of monastic life, such as Iona, kept details of the travels of monks who set out for the north. This may be said to be borne out by the story of Orlyg:

'Orlyg was the name of a man who was the son of Hrapp, the son of Bjorn Cuna; he was brought up by the Holy Patrick, Bishop of Sodor. He conceived the desire to go to Iceland, and asked the Bishop St. Patrick who had brought him up that he would make provision for his setting out. The Bishop provided him with wood, suitable for building a church and a plenarium and an iron bell, a golden penny and consecrated earth, to put under the corner pillars. Afterwards the Bishop told him that he should take land where he should see two mountains rising out of the sea, and rear his dwelling under the southernmost mountain; in either mountain there should be a valley, and there should he take up his abode, and let build there a church and should consecrate it to the Saint Columba'.

Orlyg put to sea and almost passed clear to the west of Iceland. He managed, however, to get into Patrick's fjord in the north-west and named it after his foster father, the Bishop. The next summer he sailed south and west about the land and eventually recognized the hills, as what we now call the Esjar opposite Reykjavik. Now unless we credit the Bishop with very powerful second-sight, which is of course possible, it is clear that he had before him a description of this very place and chose it out of others as a suitable site for his foster son's home. This must have taken place between about 875 A.D. and 900 A.D., nearly a hundred years in fact since the visit of

Dicuil's Irishmen. It is a nice, sunny, grassy place beneath hills which look like the Cuillins of Skye, and I am not surprised that Patrick suggested it. There are no nearby icecaps and it is sheltered from the north.

In another place we find: 'Ketil dwelt at Kirkby [Kirkjubæ] —there the Papar had formerly had their abode, and no heathen men might settle there'. But Kirkby is high up on the east coast of Iceland and moreover is ten miles inland. It is clear from this, and from the details about Papyle and Papos, that we may expect to hear of traces of ancient monastic settlement being found all round the east, south and west coasts of Iceland. What are we to think about the medieval monastery on Flatey, in Breithifjorthur; was not the site for this almost certainly chosen on the knowledge of the former existence of a Celtic one?

The whole matter boils down to this. For hundreds of years people from Scotland and Ireland had been going to Iceland. At least one of them had been blown over to Greenland. The Norsemen did not go to Iceland until they had been settled in the Hebrides and Ireland for many years. When it was decided that Iceland was worth attention as a home, many of the settlers came from the Hebrides. Some were even told exactly where to live. The permanent settlement of Iceland is almost certainly due to the information obtained about it by the people of Britain in earlier days. The picture cannot be elaborated to any great extent until places like Kirkby and Papyle have been properly examined. Is it, however, beyond the bounds of probability that some Celtic people, not necessarily monks, but perhaps genuine farmers, were living in Iceland at the time of the Settlement? Who, for instance, were the 'cave dwellers'? 'Torfi slew the men of Kropp, twelve of them together. He also promoted the slaughter of the Holmsmen [Islanders], and he was at Hellisfitar, with Illugi the Black, and Sturla the Gothi, when eighteen cavemen were slain there' (Torfi was the great-grandson of Orlyg from the Hebrides).

Of course, these may have been brigands, or outlaws, but these things took place at a comparatively early date. I am far from convinced that, because Naddod the Viking went ashore on the east coast and to the top of a high mountain from which he could not see any smoke or sign of habitation, there may not have been Celts living elsewhere. The silence in the *Landnamabok* may just cover a feeling of shame, because the Viking settlers had murdered the lot. The passage quoted above reads very much like an account of the efforts of the early Tasmanian farmers against the Aborigines, and is quite typical of what apparently happened when the Norsemen reached America. These were rough days, when your nearest neighbour might burn your house over your head at night because of some rude remark you made when you were drunk at a feast. It was much better not to have any scruffy looking men living around in earth houses or on islands. Why, they might take your lambs, or anything.

If people had been going to Iceland more or less continuously over so long a period of years, it must be possible to recognize some signs of their visits. The bells and books and croziers of the *Landnamabok* suggest that the monastic settlements were not without the usual equipment of religious establishments. The monks did not go to Iceland just to sit and dream on the cliff top, or pick the lice from their shirts when they became numerous. They went there to worship God, as well as to meditate. Some settled on islands where in summer they could be sure of a plentiful supply of sea-birds and their eggs. Others, such as those at Kirkby and Papos, must have taken their livestock with them and done some farming, as well as continuing their religious devotions. Monks had to have food like anyone else although some hermits are said to have lived on herbs alone. Places like Iona had their farming aspect as well as their religious one. It is, I think, safe to argue that Kirkby must have been maintained all the year round. It is not the only Kirkby. There is another in the Faeroe Islands, on the grassy slope of a hill just above the sea. It is much the same type of site as that to which Patrick sent Orlyg.

Now the island sites round our own shores had monastic settlements on them in great numbers. Some, like Skellig Michael on the coast of Kerry and Eileann-nan-Naoimh in the Firth of Lorne, are perched on precipitous islets. Others, like those on the Seven Hogs off Tralee and Pabay beside Skye, are low grassy islands on which sheep and cattle can graze. There is no certainty that one site would be chosen rather than another. Any island round the coasts of Iceland might have been chosen for a hermitage. There is one group of islands, however, off the south-western shore, which bears a name directly connecting them with Britain. These are the Vestmannæjar, or Westman Islands. Westmen were the men of the British Isles. The *Landnamabok* has a story recording the naming of these islands, but it has the appearance of being invented to account for their name. Ingolf, the first Norse settler, went there with a friend named Hjorleif, so the story goes. The ships were separated and came ashore in different places. Hjorleif was murdered by his Irish slaves, who fled to the Westman Islands. Ingolf later found Hjorleif murdered; he climbed a hill, looked out to sea and saw the Islands, and jumped to the conclusion that the thralls had murdered Hjorleif and had fled there. He went out to the islands, found the slaves and slew them all. 'And these islands where the slaves were slain have since been called the Westman's Islands, because those who were slain were Westmen'. This story might be true, but it sounds like a fairy tale. The islands are more than sixty miles from the place where Hjorleif was killed and out of sight round a bend of the coast.

The Westman Islands are famous for their puffins. Thousands upon thousands breed there. Many are caught by fowlers in nets like lacrosse sticks, and dried for food in winter. The oily skins are used as firelighters. One of the best fowling grounds is the Heimaklettr, which forms the north side of Heimaey harbour. It is a high crag with its only

H

approach up a series of dangerous cliff ledges. Many of the
thralls are said to have jumped from it into the sea. There are
wooden ladders placed now in the most difficult part of the
ascent. As I went up one of them on the worst bit, I noticed
foot and hand holds cut in the soft rock. Beside them was a
cross, some two foot long, with expanded ends to its extrem-
ities. This cross is roughly done. It was put there with extreme
difficulty by a man suspended hundreds of feet above the sea.
It may be medieval, for it is impossible to be sure. It is, however, very like the early Christian crosses found in Ireland and
Western Scotland. One, on a slab with Hiberno-Saxon lettering of about the seventh century, was found at Barnakill,

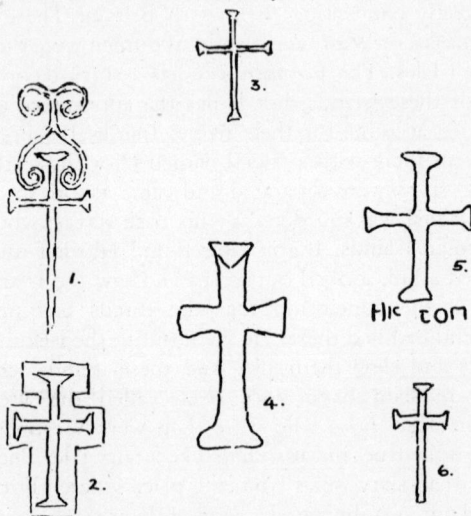

ROCK-CUT CROSSES OF CELTIC TYPE

1. Papil, Shetland (after P. Moor and J. Stewart) *c.* 8th—9th century A.D.
2. Pabbay, Barra near ancient chapel and another stone with 'Pictish'
   symbols and similar cross. *c.* 7th—8th century.
3. Hynish, Tiree (after Lacaille).
4. Heimaclettr, Westman Islands, Iceland.
5. Barnakill, Argyll (after Lacaille) *c.* 7th century.
6. Ard a Mhorain, North Uist.

north of the Crinan Canal; there is another at Ach-na-Cille, Obimore in Knapdale. Both places, by their names, indicate the former presence of early churches. There is another at Hynish in Tiree, two on Pabay in the Sound of Harris, and a sixth at Papil in Shetland supports a stone engraved with the figures of hooded priests. Perhaps the most interesting of all is cut on a rock at high tide mark in North Uist above a well which rises in the beach.

The whole series belongs to the days between St. Columba's mission and the coming of the Vikings. It seems most probable that this Icelandic cross belongs to the same period. It is a piece of magic put there to scare off demons from the climber. Someone on Skellig Michael climbed out to the end of a pinnacle of rock and carved one there for a similar purpose. Foot-holds are also cut in the rock ascent to the monastery on the cliff top. Another hint that this cross may be the work of the Celtic monks or Papar, is to be found in the ruins on the summit, almost invisible in the coarse grass, of a small round building, which looks uncommonly like a bee-hive hut, such as you can still see standing on Skellig Michael or Eileann-nan-Naoimh. This is no definite proof, but somebody ought to dig out that ruin. There is probably very little in it, but the missing piece of evidence may be there.

There are other mysterious things in Iceland which await explanation. In the district opposite the Westman Islands there is a large number of artificial caves of high antiquity known as Hellir. Every now and then a new one is found. In *Merlin's Island*, I gave a rough plan of two of them, which opened into the side of a little grassy valley above the river at Ægisidu. They look so like a beehive hut and small rectangular chapel cut in the rock, that it makes one wonder whether they are not a monastic adaptation to suit the colder climate.

Before leaving this fascinating series of problems, it is of interest to note that if Gunnar of Lithend really lived at Litherendi, as is told in the famous *Niala*,* he must have often

* Dasent, *The Story of Burnt Nial*

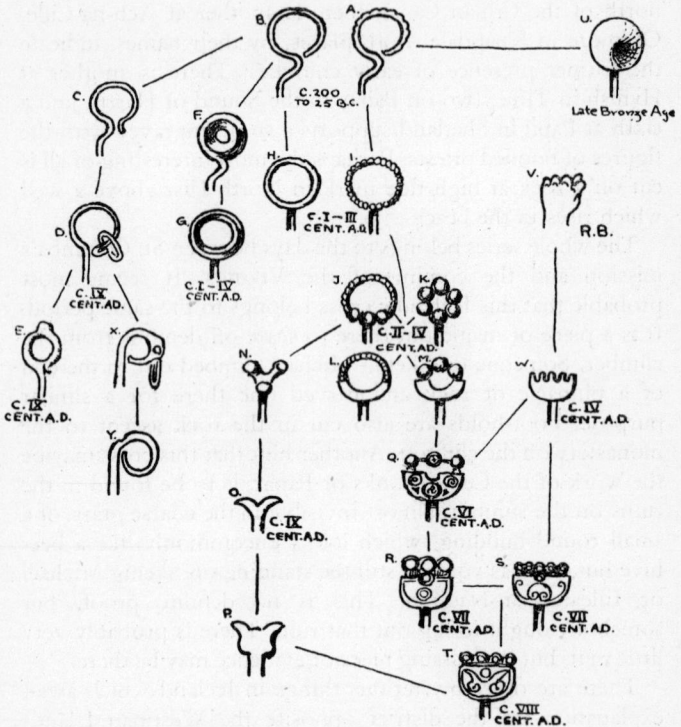

SOME LINES OF EVOLUTION OF PINS

A *and* B. Common type of Early Iron Age pin found at numerous places in Southern Britain.

C.   Bonchester; Abernethy.

D.   Ballinderry Crannog, Ireland.

E.   Mote of Mark.

F.   Hagbourne Hill, Berks.; Dunagoil; Traprain (early); Carsphain.

G.   Traprain; Dun Add; Ness Broch, Caithness; Gallanach, Oban; etc.

H.   North and South Uist with Broch pottery; Traprain to 3rd century A.D.

I.   Traprain 2nd century A.D.

J.   Late Roman temple, Lydney, Gloucester; Traprain; North Berwick; Broch of Bowermadden, Caithness; Sandy, Beds.; Newnham,

Continued on page 87

looked out at the Westman Islands and admired perhaps their rugged outlines, rising like sharks' fins from the ocean's rim. He sounds that sort of man.

It is not very encouraging to note how very little we know about the conditions of life in Scotland at this time. In the Chronicles we can get glimpses of the movements of savage armies, but of the everyday life of the ordinary man we know practically nothing.

As far as I can judge from the results obtained, often a long time ago, in excavating brochs, some of these were occupied for a long period. It is true that Viking burials have been found, which had utilized ruins as if they were cairns. This does not necessarily mean that all brochs had been deserted long before the coming of the Norsemen. They could have been destroyed in tribal wars, or by an insurrection of serfs, or by raiders from Ireland. Their people may have died of a pestilence and the survivors may have moved elsewhere. They could even have tumbled in through faulty construction. On the other hand, two of them, the brochs of Burrian in Orkney

---

Cambridge. It is not known how late the temple at Lydney continued in use. It is possible that it survived into the 6th century A.D.

K. Traprain.
L. Late Roman temple, Lydney; Traprain.
M. Traprain.
N. Bruthach a Tuath, Benbecula, with Broch pottery.
O. Ballinderry Crannog, Ireland; Broch of Burrian, Orkney.
P. Broch of Burrian, Orkney.
Q. Norrie Law, Fife. Has Cross in front and Pictish symbols on back.
R. Pabbay, Barra.
S. Craigywarren, Antrim.
T. Urquhart, Elgin.
U. Late Bronze Age 'Sunflower' pin from Denmark and Ireland.
V. Romano-British charm against the 'Evil Eye'.
W. Late Roman temple at Lydney probably later than 367 A.D.
X. Ireland.
Y. Quoybanks, Mainland, Orkney.

Partly based on the work of the late Reginald Smith and others. The diagram shows clearly that simple types may remain, like B, C and D, in use for many centuries and are unreliable for dating purposes. On the other hand elaborate examples can probably be dated with considerable accuracy.

and Dun Fiardhart in Skye, contained objects which are probably as late as the seventh century. I know nothing about the levels at which objects were found at Burrian. The things however, which were recovered are most interesting, and are illustrated in the *Proceedings of the Antiquaries of Scotland* for 1872. There is a phalange bone of an ox, engraved with symbols like those of the Pictish stones. This is certainly later than St. Colomba. There is a little iron bell, probably very like the one Bishop Patrick gave to Orlyg. Finally there is a large series of bone pins of various shapes; one at least of which is probably later than the Anglo-Saxon wars of Ecgfrith. Perhaps one or two diagrams of pins (page 86) will explain the significance of these better than a long description. It is clear to me, from a study of Scottish pins which I was persuaded to undertake by Sir Lindsay Scott, that there was a very close connexion between Scotland and Ireland throughout the Dark Ages. Again and again one can trace the development of the forms of Scottish pins only by making use of Irish specimens to fill the gaps. Pins are very common in Scotland and when their development sequences have been worked out, they should be quite as useful for dating purposes as brooches are in the Iron, Roman, Saxon and Viking periods. I only show a very few types here, but I hope in time to carry the study much further.

So far then we appear to have evidence that farming and hunting men were still using the brochs after the days of St. Colomba. They were also in frequent contact with Ireland. Other communities were living in monastic groups all round the coasts. There were, however, people living in hill forts, such as Dun Add, where 'Pictish symbols' and other evidence of a seventh century or later occupation have been found. Perhaps most people lived in hill forts or cliff castles. I hardly think, however, that this was the case. There are too many ancient sites of tiny churches which look like those of people living in small clachans, or villages. All clerics were not monks, probably more were serving the daily needs of the

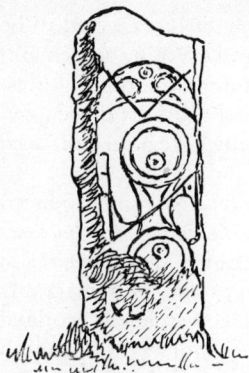

AN EXAMPLE OF
'PICTISH SYMBOLS'
The 'Clach Ard' at Tote in Skye.
*A similar stone on Pabbay, Barra,
has a cross 'potent' standing on the
upper crescent.*

people. As far as one can judge, the age was not particularly restless. The only monastic settlement to meet with misfortune was the one on Eigg, where the monks were attacked by raiders. These are described as Lochlanach, which is usually translated as Vikings. Probably in this case they were Saxon pirates. This occurred in 617 A.D. The site has not been identified but there are ruins of a monastic settlement on Canna. If one reads the accounts of the early Viking attacks on the British Isles, it is clear that these came as a great surprise to comparatively peaceful people. Had everybody been living in forts and in a perpetual state of war, this could hardly have been the case. People were just caught completely unprepared. One hears of how the heathen burned this and that place, but not of how they were beaten off from so and so's dun or castle. When they had to fight, it was always against a field army which somebody had collected. Kings, however, made gifts of duns to bishops and so on. The duns must have been occupied, but perhaps only as stockyards.

It would not be difficult to learn a great deal more about this early Christian age. I think that attempts should be made to find and excavate ancient village sites in the neighbourhood of the old Cilles, or chapels, such as Barnakill and Ach-na-Cille in Argyll. These names are so numerous that the task should not be difficult. Such a deserted site might be expected to be later than St. Columba and earlier than the Viking settlement. That is roughly from the seventh to mid-ninth centuries. Very many of such sites, however, are of course still occupied and those that are not need not necessarily have been destroyed by the Norsemen.

Recently the Scientific Research Fund of Norway produced a five volume survey of *Viking Antiquities in Great Britain and Ireland*. Volume V gives a list of the British antiquities taken home as loot and found in Norway, and is remarkably instructive. A very large number of objects stolen in Scotland and Ireland were taken home to western Norway in the ninth and tenth centuries. Of these Celtic objects, the majority are pieces of beautiful and elaborate bronze-work torn off ecclesiastical valuables. There are fragments of shrines and bits of book covers, mostly cut up and made into brooches. There is even a censer and two complete little shrines. There are numerous fine bronze buckets with enamelled human figures to support their handles, and there are pans and skillets modelled on original Romano-British designs. As far as one can see, almost all this was obtained in the western lands and comparatively little from England. It shows how very rich the churches and monasteries were in beautiful objects in the years between St. Patrick and the new heathen kings who settled in Dublin. How many beautiful books, like those of Kells, Lindisfarne, and Durrow were torn up to make ornaments for peasant women in Norway we will never know, but there must have been a great many. It is rather wonderful that any have survived to the present day.

It is thought that the raiders were preceded in the Orkneys by comparatively peaceful peasant farmers, and that they found few people living there. If this is true, something caused the migration of the men of the Orkneys southward into Scotland itself. The cause may possibly have been another wet period, which is believed to have occurred about 800 A.D. It is hard to believe that the Orkneys were completely depopulated.

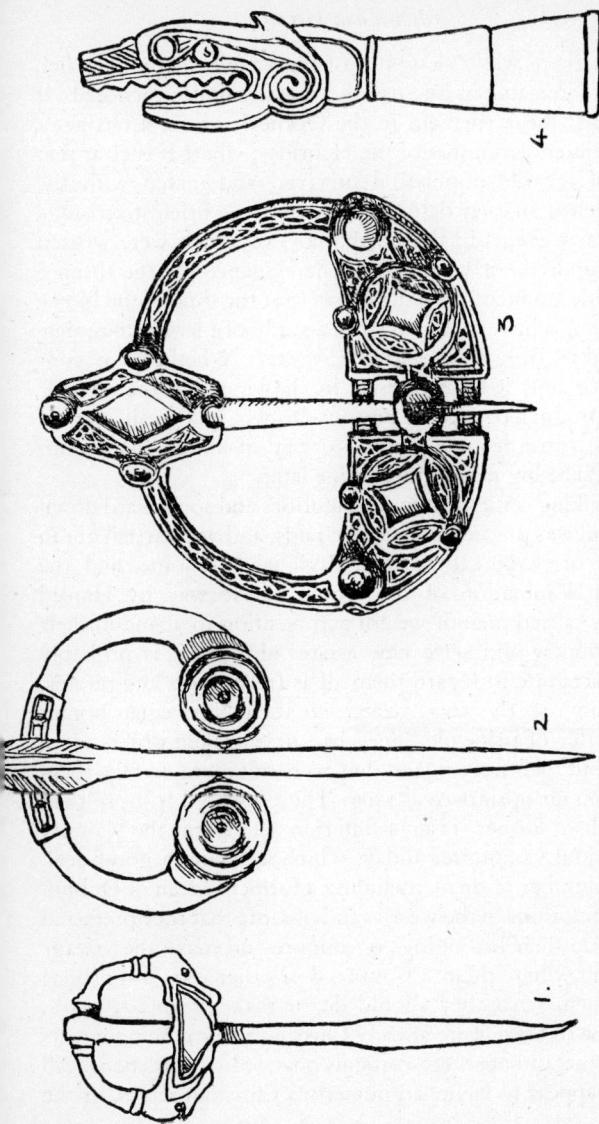

EXAMPLES OF VIKING LOOT FROM THE BRITISH ISLES FOUND IN NORWAY

(Based on Jan Petersen)

1. Bronze pin. 2 and 3. Penannular brooches (2 is 4½ inches long). 4. End of a drinking horn.

1, 2 and 3 found in 9th century graves.

Possibly there was a slaughter of the people there, of which no record remains in history, and the remainder then fled. If this is so, the settlement in the Orkneys was of a character quite different from that of the Hebrides, where it is clear that many of the old population survived and mixed with the Norsemen at an early date. We have only the briefest accounts of any early events in the north, most of which were written down hundreds of years later. The evidence for the absence of a Celtic population in the Orkneys at the time of the Norse settlement, which is drawn from a study of place names, may be found in Brogger's *Ancient Emigrants*. Whether it is conclusive or not, it is of interest in showing that the settlers, whom Brogger regards as peasant-farmers in a small way of business, came from western Norway in about the eighth century. The big pirate chiefs came later.

The Viking settlement in the Hebrides and southward down to Ireland was preceded by savage raids, and was carried out in the face of perpetual warfare. Civil war at home, and the eventual domination of the whole of Norway by Harold Fairhair, caused men of wealth and position to abandon their home country and seize new estates abroad. It is probably quite inaccurate to regard them all as freebooters and pirates. Very many, so the sagas relate, left their Norwegian homes on a matter of principle. They had never taken orders from anyone but their fathers, and they were not going to take them now from an upstart over-king. They resented it more than an English farmer resents interference from the County Agricultural Committee today, which is saying a good deal. Quite a number of them, including a former Queen of Dublin, found conditions in the west so full of strife that they preferred to pack up their belongings once more and make the voyage to Iceland, where there was no civil or other war, and no one to tell them what they should do or make them pay taxes. Not a few of these were already Christians from their contacts in the west. Others were certainly married to Christians. All of them appear to have had numerous Christian slaves, or the children of Christian captives, in their retinue. It is not necessary to quote long passages from the sagas to illustrate all this. It has frequently been done before and in any case every educated man ought to read the saga literature, which is quite as fine as that of ancient Greece and moreover concerns our own land and ancestors. If men take an interest in the breeding of their stock, they should also trouble to learn about their own.

When we come to study the archaeology of this period, we find it to be remarkably patchy. The graves of many Norsemen and women have been opened. Plenty of ninth and tenth century Viking battle-axes, spears and swords, knives and bridle-bits, weights and balances, tortoise brooches, pins and

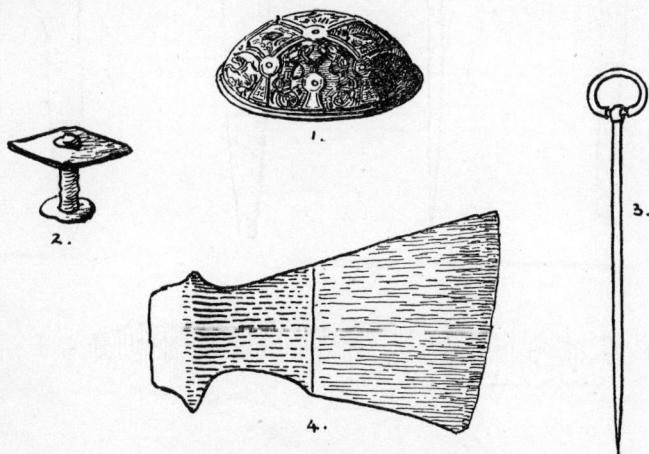

TYPICAL VIKING OBJECTS OF THE
NINTH CENTURY A.D.

1. Bronze 'Tortoise' brooch (*c.* 4 inches). Specimens of this form of tortoise brooch have been found in Norway, Orkney, Lewis and Ireland. They were probably made in Norway.
2. Iron clinch nail from a boat (*c.* 1 inch head).
3. Bronze pin with loose ring head (*c.* 4 inches).
4. Iron battle-axe. From a burial in Skye (7½ inches long).

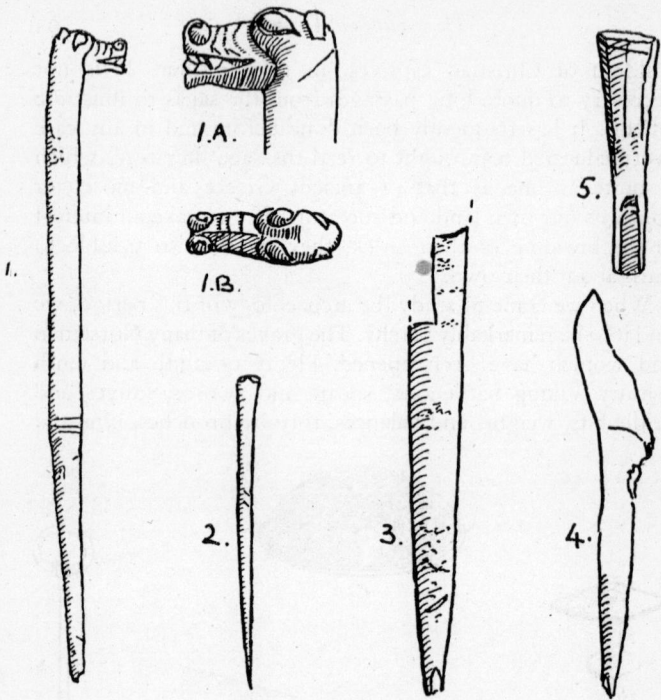

1.A.

1.B.

1.

2.

3.

4.

5.

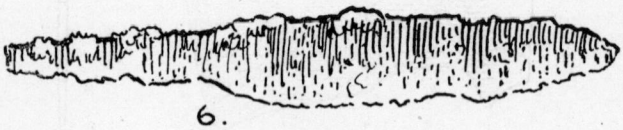

6.

0.   1.   2.
INCHES

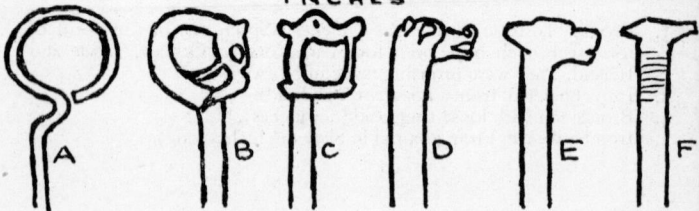

A   B   C   D   E   F

padlocks, beads and the ends of drinking horns, have been dug up and preserved in museums. Hoards of looted and broken-up silver ornaments have been found, together with many English and even Arabic coins. Stolen pieces of Celtic bronze-work have turned up in several graves. The picture of the home life of the people is, however, almost a complete blank. Rectangular stone foundations of farm buildings, dating probably from the tenth century, have been excavated at Jarlshoff in Shetland. In the west of Scotland no work of any kind has really been done. A kitchen midden at Galson in Lewis has been explored, and proved to contain coins, pins, and combs of the tenth century. I have myself stumbled on a small earth house in the talus at the foot of a cliff on Kerrera which dates from the same period. No one, however, has found the sites of the farms of the Norse settlers. The difficulty is that the Norsemen habitually built their halls of wood; and the remains of a wooden house, even if placed on a stone foundation, are not easy to detect. Not only is this the case, but also, since most of these farms would undoubtedly have been situated near good farming land, the sites have no doubt been permanently occupied ever since. Even the stone

---

1—6.	Objects from an Earth-house on Kerrera. (1A and 1B enlarged).
1.	Carved bone pin ornamented in a style common in Celtic lands at the time of the early Viking wars (*c.* 9th century).
2.	Small type of bone pin also found at Galson in Lewis with coin of Edgar (957–75 A.D.)
3—5.	Bone pins and wedge.
6.	Typical iron knife of Viking age.
A—F.	Evolution of Beast-headed pin.
A.	Iron or Bronze wire pin type common all over British Isles from about 250 B.C. for perhaps two centuries.
B *and* C.	Bronze pins derived from A and found in Ireland (after Armstrong).
D.	Kerrera pin.
E.	Bronze pin from Jarlshof, Shetland (after A. O. Curle). (*c.* 10th century.)
F.	Debased form in bone from hut-circle at Ackergill, Wick. (*P.S.A.S.* 1911).

SEE ILLUSTRATION ON OPPOSITE PAGE

foundation would have been utilized for some other purpose. There is another reason why the sites have not been observed. The Norsemen did not use pottery vessels at the time of the settlement. It is a curious fact that, although the Norwegians made continuous use of elaborate and often highly decorative pottery right up to the sixth or seventh century A.D., yet in the ninth century they were using none at all, unless it happened to be the crocks of the peoples living near them. The midden of the Norse farm in the Hebrides will not then be crammed with broken potsherds of a characteristic type. If there is pottery at all, it will be that of the descendants of the broch people. This phase of culture has survived in Iceland right up to the present day. You can still go into the farm house at Keldur, possibly in part the same building from which, the saga says, Ingialld refused to go with Flossi's band to burn Nial in his house at Bergthorsnoll, and see the mass of wooden tubs and buckets, cups and boxes, which were used by the Norsemen instead of pots and pans. Where possible they supplemented these with bronze cauldrons, buckets and skillets, bought or looted overseas.

I have seen two Scottish sites which may date back to the days of the Norse settlement. One of these was at Keoldale in Sutherland, within a short distance of a rifled barrow, which appears to have been that of a woman provided with tortoise brooches and padlocked chests. The second is at Hogh Bay in Coll, where the once fertile farming land has been overwhelmed by drifting sand. Here in 1934 the plan of the lower courses of a rectangular building 27 feet by 12 feet could still be seen. It was not as long as a Hebridean blackhouse and had no rounded corners. The midden outside had weathered away and, amid the sheep bones and shells, lay scraps of iron, lead net sinkers, clinch nails from old boats used as firewood, pieces of double-sides combs, ends of padlocks, iron arrowheads, broken buckles, and pieces of glazed pottery probably traded up from England in the early Middle Ages. There were also a few scraps of coarse hand-made pottery ornamented with the impression of bird bones, which are unlike anything else I have seen. I take them to be Hebrido-Norse pottery of the early Middle Ages. They seem to copy the shapes of twelfth- or thirteenth-century jugs.

The true hall of the Norsemen in Iceland is now well-known. By a fortunate chance, I was there at the time when several such halls were being excavated in 1939. These halls, which stood on what had once been fertile land far inland up Thjorsadalr, had been abandoned and covered by ash when Hecla was in eruption. They are very long buildings, with turf walls which had once been lined with boards. They had been low roofed with a long fireplace down the centre. Rows of small posts, found for two-thirds of the length and away from the walls and parallel to the sides, indicated the edges of raised sleeping platforms, leaving a large open space down the middle of the building. Smoke from the open fires no doubt filtered out of the roof through louvres or lumms. They were sometimes over eighty feet in length. Not a scrap of pottery of any kind was found in the early ones; nothing but a few old knife blades, beads or spindle whorls and sometimes pieces of combs. We may expect precisely the same thing from the remains of a Norse hall in Skye or Barra. When the home of Sommerled is found 'in the Dales', which is thought to mean Knapdale, it is improbable that it will contain objects of great intrinsic value. Does the name Knapdale itself retain a trace of Ptolemy's Epidium, the original designation of Kintyre?

The names of Norse earls or kings of the islands show a mixture of Celtic with the Gaelic. There was an Earl Gilli, for instance, in Coll, who may have been a direct ancestor of Sommerled, Lord of the Isles. Not far from Arinagour, the port of Coll, Beveridge noted a Cnoc Gillibreidhe, which he describes as 'not a rock fort, but on comparatively high arable ground. It now consists of two enclosures of large stones (that to the west measuring some fifty feet in diameter) containing the foundations of a number of small separate buildings, some circular, but others apparently rectangular'. If this site has any

RECONSTRUCTIONS OF NORSE HALLS

A. Type used in tree-less country with turf walls and roofing. Based on
    the excavations in Thjorsadalur in Iceland and Brough of Birsay in
    Orkney.

B. Type used in wooded country with plank walls and shingles on the
    roof. Based on the Trelleborg excavations and the Northumbrian
    'Hog-back' gravestones.

NOTE. *The Hebridean 'Black-house', though it resembles the Norse houses in some
respects, is entirely different in construction and is probably a hybrid. In Greenland
the houses were protected from the cold by long entrance passages.*

connexion with Earl Gilli, whose name was probably Gil Brigid, it should be dated about 1000 A.D. This place ought to be properly examined, for it might give us some important information.

We have now dealt with almost all that is known about the Norse settlements in Western Scotland. They included most of the islands and various fertile patches such as parts of Ardnamurchan[6], Kintyre and Galloway. It is improbable that the former occupants were either killed off, or were entirely enslaved. It was the usual form of early conquest settlement by force and dominated by sword and spear. Many people were, however, taken prisoner in war and were enthralled, These included the wives and daughters of petty kings, as we know from the Laxdale Saga. Olaf the Peacock, one of the characters of the story of Burnt Nial, was the son of a captive Irish princess bought at a sale in Denmark. It may confidently be assumed that the number of British captives taken to Iceland as thralls greatly exceeded the number of their owners. This is especially true of those settlers who emigrated to Iceland from the Western Isles or from Ireland. Some people of Celtic birth went there of their own free will: an instance of this is Kalaman from the Hebrides. In spite of this very large proportion of Gaelic - and perhaps Welsh-speaking persons among the settlers in Iceland, there are less than a dozen Celtic words in the Icelandic language and place-names. This makes it clear that it is impossible to argue that the absence of a particular type of place-name in a district indicates the absence of people who had been using that type of language.

When I last visited Iceland, coming by way of Norway, I was very struck by the different appearance of the people in the two countries. The Icelanders as a whole bore a much greater resemblance to the peoples of the West Highlands or Ireland than they did to the Norwegians. It was not only in their appearance, but also in their way of thinking, that this came out. Old grudges of the Middle Ages were still treasured as if they had only recently been formed. One day, when we were driving through the south-western district, I was suddenly told with some heat, 'that is where they murdered the bishop'. Instantly my mind went back to a summer's afternoon ten years before on Scarif off the Kerry coast. I had climbed to the summit of the island and was sitting beside the son of the 'King', with our legs dangling over the edge of the cliff. The sea below us stretched away glassy and blue to the Statue of Liberty or to Tir-nan-Og. Suddenly he remarked, 'that is where they hanged the priest', and pointed to another nearby crag. 'Oh', I said, 'Who did that?' 'It was that bastard, Oliver Cromwell', he replied, simply. I could not imagine Oliver Cromwell rowing out to Scarif to hang a priest, so I incautiously asked how this misfortune had occurred. 'Don't you read history?' he asked fiercely, and when I said my education had been neglected, he continued, 'then how the devil should I know? It was in the time of the Danes'. You find this kind of thing just the same in Iceland. Not only that, but the old saga heroes have only died a year or two ago, or so it seems, even though Egil Skallagrimson's name now adorns your bottle of beer.

Having come home with this most unorthodox opinion of Icelanders, who are always pointed out to us as a typical example of a pure Norse race, with a pure Norse culture, I was delighted to see Professor Matthias Thordarson's report of the excavation of a medieval Icelandic graveyard in

---

THE RELATIVE DISTRIBUTION OF VIKING GRAVES IN SCOTLAND

Areas where graves are fairly numerous in Black. Isolated graves as dots.
This distribution map is undoubtedly very incomplete. Place-names suggest that there must be many more graves in the Lewis, Skye, Mull, Coll, Ardnamurchan etc. I can find record of about 70 graves in all. It is clear that the absence of graves on the Mainland of Shetland must be incorrect. Since the graves of the Viking period only give us an archaeological picture of a comparatively small area of occupation and we know that the area occupied was in reality much greater, it is only reasonable to assume that the archaeological record is equally misleading for earlier times.

SEE ILLUSTRATION ON OPPOSITE PAGE

Forntida Gardar i Island (Ancient Farms in Iceland, which contains also the excavation reports of the Thorsadalr halls). I had actually visited the graveyard and seen the skeletons uncovered. Professor Thordarson maintains that the people buried here at Skeljastathir have skull forms which are more closely allied to the old Celtic population of Ireland than to that of Norway. This is exactly what one might have expected. For generation after generation the descendants of the Norse settlers killed each other off in blood feuds. All that time, the descendants of their Celtic thralls went on quietly multiplying, so now the population is largely of the same type as you would find in Benbecula or Tiree. There is some Norse blood, but there is more of the Pict, Scot, and Beaker or Megalithic men. Yet all this time they have hardly been able to add a dozen words to the old Norse language. They did other things, however; they introduced stone killicks as anchors for boats; they introduced underground cellars or weems or fougou beneath the halls. They told stories of kelpies and water-horses, which had probably come to Britain from Mediterranean lands long before the birth of Christ. I think they modified the whole art of story-telling and bred the Saga man. Even today in their wood-carving you still see the interlacing patterns which adorned the Gospel books and were torn off by Viking pirates to make brooches for their sweethearts. The crusie lamp of Scotland and Ireland, of which the original idea had long before derived from Roman Britain, was to be seen until recently hanging in their houses.

CHAPTER SEVEN

THE SEA ROAD TO GREENLAND

THIS WAS NOT, however, the end of the adventures of the Celts. I call them Celts, although some of their ancestors had trudged across Europe from the skirts of the Alps. Others had wandered up on to the North Sea plain and had been driven by the sea into England and Scotland. Others again had coasted round perhaps even from the eastern end of the Mediterranean and had finished up in Uist. Many had been carried captive from peaceful farms in Roman Britain, to a life of servitude in Ireland. Others had wandered, spear in hand, from Somerset to Caithness. Some descendants of all these people were carried once again, between 870 and 930 A.D., six days' sail to the northward and were plumped down to herd sheep beneath icecaps and within sight of geysers and volcanoes.

The good land in Iceland is not extensive and was soon taken up. Men who came late had to take sites of little value and were soon disgruntled and dissatisfied. This led rapidly to quarrel and murder. One of those disgruntled men was Eric the Red. After many killings, his friends could no longer protect him and he was sentenced to three years' outlawry. He could be killed at sight if he remained at home. Eric was a true adventurer. Very well then, he would sail away to the west and see what sort of land Gunnbjorn had found there years before. Gunnbjorn's reefs, it was called; it did not sound prepossessing, but was Eric as ignorant as the saga makes him out to be? He was not the only man to go in search of it. In the *Landnamabok* we read: 'They went in search of Gunnbjorn-Skerries and they found a land, where Snaebjorn would not they should go ashore by night. Styrbjorn left the ship and found a treasure in a barrow and kept it hidden. Snaebjorn smote him with an axe and the treasure tumbled down. They made a scale [hall] for themselves which was soon snowed up. Thorkel, the son of Red, found that there was water on a forked pole which stood out of the scale window, and this was in the month of *goi*; and then they dug themselves out'.

Snaebjorn and Styrbjorn appear to have spent a winter on Greenland before Eric went there. It also reads as if they might have found some Eskimo ivories in a grave, although this is before the date recognized by archaeologists for Eskimo remains in southern Greenland. The discovery of Eskimo remains is attributed to Eric, and they are said to have found traces of human habitation, remnants of leather boats and stone implements, all up the south-west side of Greenland about 980 A.D. Eskimos themselves, however, are never mentioned as having been seen at such an early period.

The reason for this is, I think, clear. The weather was evidently milder at this time. Cattle could be left out all the winter in Iceland and would survive. If the weather was milder, the limits of ice would be further north, and the Eskimos would not come so far south for their specialized ice hunting. It was not until late in the thirteenth century that the ice appears to have started creeping south again. Eric returned with good reports of the possibilities of farming in Greenland. He called it, as it is said, 'Greenland' to encourage people to go there. About 985 A.D., a fleet of twenty-five ships sailed from Borgarfirth and Broadfirth to colonize the country. Fourteen of them got there; some were lost and some were driven back. In these fourteen ships not a few of the crews and passengers would have been of Celtic stock. In their memories were still to be found traces of the stories of the 'Land of Women', far to the west of Ireland and of Tir-nan-Og, the land of youth, beyond the sunset. They may even have handed down, generation after generation, the story of Cormac and the myriads of stinging creatures. They were soon to find the creatures for themselves.

This land beyond the sunset is even today not so inhospitable as people think. In the south the modern Greenlanders

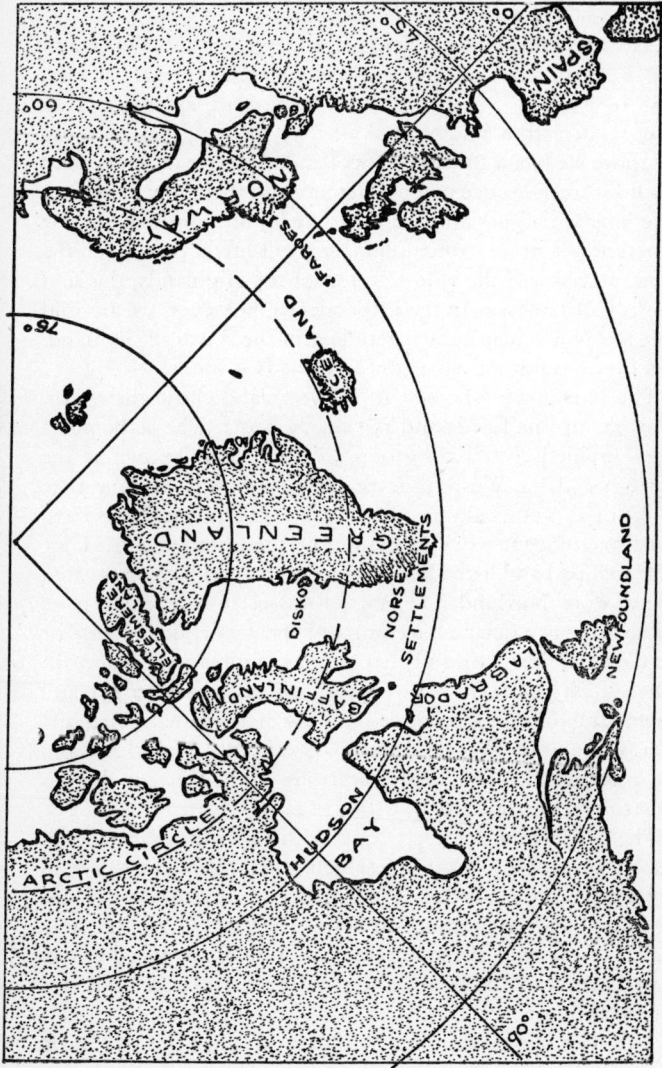

THE RELATIVE SIZES AND POSITIONS OF THE COUNTRIES IN THE NORTHERN SEAS

breed sheep and cattle. There are wide grassy hill slopes and valley floors. In some places there are birch thickets. In the days of Eric, all this would have been more extensive. It is a more attractive land to look at than Iceland, for the rocks are those we know in western Scotland. A native of Sutherland would scarcely notice much difference and then only in degree. The hills are higher and the rocks stick out more sharply, the vegetation is more stunted, but the plant life is very much the same. In place of the wild red deer of the Highlands, the land was full of reindeer. In the Orkney saga, however, we are told that the Norsemen hunted reindeer in the north of Scotland, and they would not have confused the two kinds.

The Norsemen who settled in Greenland chose their farm lands far up the fjords and not on the coast. The settlements were divided into two groups, which were known as the Eastern and the Western Settlements, although the one they spoke of as west is almost north of the other. The Danes have done magnificent work in examining these settlements. They have mapped and listed hundreds of farms and have excavated many. Poul Nørlund and Aage Roussel in particular have published very detailed accounts of their work in *Meddelelser om Gronland*, but Nørlund also wrote a summary of his work called *Viking Settlers in Greenland*, which is easy to get and fascinating to read. The whole story is a most dramatic struggle against the gradual deterioration of farming conditions and the interruption of communications with Europe due to governmental stupidity.

The Greenland colonists took with them that same north European farming tradition which still lingers on today in Iceland and the Hebrides. It included a reliance to some extent on fishing and on hunting. In essentials it was much the same as that of the men of the brochs; rather more advanced it may have been, and perhaps a little more comfortable, but not appreciably so.

A crofter of two hundred years ago would have seen little strange to him in an eleventh-century hall at Brattahlid in

Greenland. The sheep he would know well from St. Kilda. The cows would seem rather small. The ponies were just like his own. The house was not unlike his own home, although he might be surprised that the cows were kept in another building and not allowed to see the fire. The boats were quite familiar. There were no pottery craggans, but only soapstone bowls and wooden tubs. It was strange, perhaps, not to see a caschrom leaning up against the wall, but the climate would not let the Norsemen grow corn. There were no iron crusies either, and only soapstone lamps in their stead. The people, too, had a novel way of cleaning themselves by steaming in a hot room; a trick which, had he known it, had drifted all that way from ancient Rome. The folk themselves were just like his own, but they were terribly quarrelsome. He himself had been out with the '45 maybe, but he had never seen people who would cut each other down with an axe over the price of a bit of an old boat. Ah well, it was a long way away, 1,400 miles perhaps in an undecked vessel. Even the priest himself could hardly read in his books. They might be a bit outlandish, but they had the ceilidh in the evening just as he did himself. The very tales they told were much the same as he had often heard over the fire. There was the spaewife too just the same as she was at home, but she would be wearing a grand dress and would not be in the least afraid of the priest. The men would be away in the summer, perhaps; far off to the north they would go, killing great sea-beasts with long ivory tusks in their mouths. When they were away, they would sometimes meet little men in skin boats with ugly, grinning faces. Well, he knew who *they* were, for had not his own father caught one of them, who showed him where the gold was hidden up in the old dun? As far as I can see, there was precious little difference in it all except the winter's cold. The only real difference between it and the life in the Hebrides in the second century A.D. was probably the shape of the house, and the Christian religion. To go even further back, it differed only very little from life in Bronze Age Scotland, when men were often coming and going up and down the sea lochs on errands of peace or war. They did just the same in Greenland, and there was always the chance of a ship coming in from far overseas, with remarkable news of strange doings in unknown and scarcely imaginable lands.

Quite a lot of documentary information concerning Greenland has survived to the present day. There are sagas, such as *Eric the Red*, *Flomanna* and *Fosttraedra* [*Fosterbrothers*,] *Saga*, official records or annals of Skalaholt and the *Flatey-Book*, and even a detailed report listing the names and situations of settlements, with geographical descriptions of the country. This is the one of Ivar Baardson, which Bjorn and Arngrimur Jonnson copied from an ancient manuscript in the middle of the seventeenth century. Ivar's mid-fourteenth-century account is so detailed that many of the old Norse ruins, both farms and churches, have been identified from it, and the Norse names of fjords and even of mountains have been re-discovered. The farm of Eric the Red at Brattahlid has been found and excavated, and so has the cathedral church at Gardar, with several others besides. Infinitely more is known about the Norse settlement in Greenland than is known about the west of Scotland. I am by no means sure that a somewhat similar reconstruction could not be carried out in the Western Isles. It would need, however, much scholarship and field work.

The old sea routes to Greenland, something approaching 'Sailing Directions', have been preserved in the *Landnamabok* There are various versions of the *Landnamabok*, but the most detailed instruction runs something like this: 'Leaving Hernum [near Bergen in Norway] and sailing westward to Hvarf [near Cape Farewell in Greenland] the course is north round Shetland with the land just in sight, thence southward of the Faeroe Islands with half the hills in view and then south of Iceland so that the sea birds from it and the whales can be seen. [This distance is given as twelve sea miles in one place and forty-eight in another.] After this you come to the high land in Greenland. The day before another high mountain is seen, which is called Hvidserk [White shirt—probably near Cape Farewell] and between these two high mountains lies Herjolfsness with the harbour of Sand near it. Sand is the universal harbour for Norwegians and merchants.

'From Stad [in Norway] to Horn [in Iceland, near Papyle] is seven days' and nights' sailing.

'The ancient course from Iceland to Greenland was two days' and nights' sailing from Snaefelsness due west to Gunnbjorn's skerries, which are halfway to the Greenland Settlements. The later course, after the ice had come south from the sea bays and made it no longer safe to go close to the skerries, was a day's and a night's sailing just south of west to avoid the ice and then one day and one night to the north west coming in under Hvarf. The shortest voyage from Snaefelsness to the Greenland Settlements takes four days.'

It is not possible to lay either of these courses today, for the ice comes down well below the latitude of Hvarf. I have paraphrased these directions to make them easier to understand.

There are two other interesting notes in the *Landnamabok*. One says: 'There are four (or two) days' sailing from Langaness [the north easterly horn of Iceland] to Svalbard northwards in the sea bay'. Svalbard is probably Frans Joseph Fjord in East Greenland. It is possible to reach this fjord in most years now through the pack ice, but in 1923 we were unable to get through in a motor sealer. The second states: 'From Reykjaness [the south-west horn of Iceland] to Jolduhlaup in Ireland is five (or three) days and nights at sea'. Jolduhlaup (the Mare's Leap) could hardly be reached in a five days' passage. Perhaps this entry refers to the Butt of Lewis. The Mare's Leap has not yet been identified. Gustav Storm places it near Lough Foyle. This may be correct, in which case the distance appears to be wrongly recorded.

The vessels used by the Norse voyagers in these days were not of course the great war galleys which are well-known from

the ship-burials in Norway. It is said, for instance, that it was
not safe to make the passage from Norway to the Faeroes in
one, as the sea was too wild. The round ship, as the merchant
ship was called, has not been found in a burial or illustrated in
a contemporary manuscript. She was probably not unlike a
Nordlands Jaegt, a few of which could still be seen in Norway
before 1939. She would, however, have been double-ended,
and would have been steered with a single quarter-rudder on
the starboard side. She would probably have rowing ports at
bow and stern, but not between, a single square-sail on a tall
mast stepped amidships, and a small poop deck aft, under
which privileged persons could sleep and from which the
helmsman steered. She could carry all the timber for a long
wooden hall and at least twenty persons besides. These vessels
were evidently very wet at sea, for we hear frequent mention
of heavy work at bailing. No pumps had yet been invented.
Until such vessels were decked over, they were frequently lost.
It may have been quite as safe to make the crossing from
Scotland to Iceland in a curragh as in a Norse merchant. In
many cases the trouble was probably the overloading. Even
in these days, I have seen small Norwegian sealing ships in the
far north so piled up with barrels, hut frames, store chests,
paraffin drums, and the like, that one wondered why the sea
did not claw the whole lot overboard and how the crew
managed to get from one end of the vessel to the other.

I am sure the passage out to Iceland with house timber,
which is so often mentioned in the sagas, was a most risky
undertaking. When to this were added thralls, cattle, sheep
and horses, it is amazing how the job was managed at all.
No wonder that when Flossi, the burner of Nial, sailed from
Norway in a ship which he was told was unseaworthy, he was
never heard of again. He was fetching house timber. She was
probably piled so high that the crew could not get at the
halliards to reef the sail. A great square-sail like that takes some
handling. It is not like reefing a fore-and-after. I have talked
to men who have seen large luggers sailed under just because

they could not be reefed in a sudden squall. Inability to handle the sail of a big, overloaded, open boat in the northern seas meant death. The round Roman merchant ship was far safer, but probably not so fast. 'Overloaded, is she?' said Flossi to his anxious mate. 'Oh, well, I'm an old man now. If she founders, I couldn't care less'. And now he is out of the story!

CHAPTER EIGHT

NORSEMEN AND ESKIMOS IN GREENLAND AND AMERICA

WHILE ERIC THE RED was still alive and comfortably established in his long house at Brattahlid, an event occurred which still surprises us today. The Norsemen accidentally discovered America. Tir-nan-Og, Hy Brasil or 'Wineland the Good' was found to be really there.

It is interesting to consider the old question of what part of North America the settlers explored. This has been discussed by many writers, most of whom have neither been to Greenland, crossed Baffin Bay, nor had much knowledge of ships and seamen. I shall not bother to go into a detailed discussion of the relative value of the sources, or how many expeditions went in search of Wineland the Good. I will only say that three stories appear to me to be authentic attempts by seamen to hand down brief accounts of their voyages which might be of some future value to others. These were worked up into family histories by saga men at a later date. In one we find how Leif, the son of Eric the Red, sailing from Norway to his father's farm in West Greenland, was blown off his course and made a landfall on the coast of America at a place where grapes and self-sown wheat grew wild. He then managed to reach Greenland. He may, it seems, have touched almost any part of the American coast southward of Newfoundland and it is difficult to say more about it. The two other accounts, however, give the attempts of contemporary seamen to estimate distances. The unit of measurement was 'a day's sailing'. It is not of the slightest importance to know whether it was a day and a night's sailing, or only a day's sailing, but I have never seen any description of a Norse ship lying hove-to at night. It was a unit of measurement. Bede used it for estimating the distance from Iceland to Britain;

this he said was 'six days' sailing'. The direct distance is actually just under five hundred miles, but from port to port it may well have been nearer six hundred. It looks as if the term 'a day's sailing' represented a distance of approximately one hundred miles. At sea a vessel might cover a hundred and twenty miles at five knots in twenty-four hours with a moderate beam wind, or twenty-four miles at one knot. Her crew would say 'we took fourteen days to make the passage', or 'three weeks', or whatever the time had been. Britain, however, would remain 'six days' sailing' from Iceland even if the passage took three weeks.

Now two surviving fragments of sagas give these 'day's sailings'. Whatever their histories and backgrounds may be, it seems most probable that the estimated distances would be committed to memory and handed down correctly, together with accurate pictures of the landfalls, for the benefit of future navigators. The first account is of an accidental discovery of America ascribed to Bjarni Heriolfsson. Very briefly the story is this. His ship sailed from Norway, passed south of Cape Farewell because of fog and north wind, and made a landfall on the coast of North America. The coast was without fjords, but with small wooded hills. Bjarni was sure this was not Greenland, so sailed north for two days. Then he made another landfall on a flat shore covered with woods. He was sure that this was not Greenland either, 'as they say there are very big icebergs over there'. He therefore turned his bows from the land and sailed before a south-west wind for three days. He then sighted a mountainous country covered with glaciers. As he was sure this was not Greenland either, he would not land in spite of protests from his crew. They therefore turned out to sea again with the same south-west wind and, after four day's sailing, reached Greenland. Now this is a perfectly reasonable passage. It describes a voyage touching twice on the Labrador coast, then crossing Hudson's Strait and sighting Baffin Land icecaps, and finally covering the four hundred odd miles or so to Greenland.

The second voyage is the celebrated expedition ascribed to Thorfin Karlsefni. People have made very heavy weather of this story, largely, I believe, because they live in an age of steam navigation and find it hard to appreciate the actions of men using sail. Again I shall reduce the story to its barest elements. When Leif returned to his father, Eric, in Greenland, he brought, we are told, such glowing accounts of the land of vines and self-sown wheat which he had discovered, that others wished to see what it was like. His brother, Thorwald Erikson, fitted out an expedition, but was blown out to sea by northerly winds and never reached America at all. He returned much discouraged, after spending a miserable summer being rolled about in the North Atlantic. Thorfin Karlsefni, an enterprising merchant, next attempted the voyage. In about 1003 A.D., with an expedition of three ships, he left the Eastern Settlement near Cape Farewell, worked up the Greenland coast to the Western Settlement around the modern Godhaab, and thence to the Bear Islands, whose position is thought, from the geographical account given by Ivaar Baardson, to have been in the neighbourhood of Disko. People have been puzzled over this passage up the west coast of Greenland, because they could not appreciate that, after the experience of Thorwald, men would realize that northerly winds were to be expected in Baffin Bay at this time of year. The Norse ships were by no means close-winded and a beam wind was necessary if they were to cross to America. It was clear therefore that they must work a long way up the coast before they could hope to turn the north wind into a suitable wind for crossing. When they did make the attempt, it was only two days' sailing with a northerly wind; that is to say, approximately two hundred miles. There is one piece of Baffin Bay which fits in with this description. It is approximately two hundred miles from the vicinity of Disko south-westward to the neighbourhood of Cape Kater in Baffin Land. When they sighted the land, they put out a boat to investigate it. They found great flat stones, some of them so big that two men could lie on them with their feet touching. They called it Helluland (Stoneland). I have not been to this part of Baffin Land, but I have studied many log books kept by Whalers, who used this coast for the autumn Right whale fishing, or Rocknosing, in the early years of this century. The Admiralty Pilot, however, gives all that is required. 'Cape Kater Peninsula, from the cape to about twenty-five miles to the westward, is comparatively low-lying and undulating and, with the exception of two hills of about 150 feet (45m. 7) and 120 feet (36m. 6) respectively, is nowhere more than about 80 feet (24m. 4) high; it is very barren, and scattered over it are innumerable isolated rocks, some of colossal size'.* They then sailed south for two days and, changing course, possibly at Cape Dier, from the south to south-west, found a country overgrown with woods. They called this land Markland (Forest Land). This is again quite clear. The expedition sailed from the vicinity of Disko to Cape Kater in Baffin Land, from there they sailed southward for two days and found a wooded land. Markland can hardly be anything else but Labrador. Whether they then turned into the mouth of Hudson Bay, or went down the east coast of Labrador to Hamilton Inlet, I leave to those who know the country. One point, however, must be borne in mind when trying to establish the limits of such things as woodlands and self-sown wheat. There has certainly been some deterioration in climate since the eleventh century. All the limits of vegetation were probably further north than they are today. The expedition met both Eskimos and Indians, both of whom are still to be found in those areas which they probably reached.

There has been much speculation whether the Greenland settlers made any use of their discoveries in America. It is quite clear that they did so. They went there for timber which was not available in Greenland. In 1121 A.D. Bishop Erik Gnupsson sailed from Iceland for Wineland, presumably to attempt to convert its people, and was never heard of again.

* *Arctic Pilot,* Vol. III., 1931.

J

As late as 1347 A.D., a note in the *Flatey-Book* says: 'A ship came from Greenland. It had sailed to Markland and there were eighteen men on board'. The same event is related in the Skalholt annals, which add that the ship was smaller than the small Icelandic merchants, had no anchor and had been driven from Markland to Iceland by a storm. In the fourteenth century the climate of Greenland became worse. Ice and, with the ice, the Eskimos came much further south than they had done since Norsemen had been settled there.

It is known that in about 1340 A.D., the Western Settlement in Greenland was found abandoned by a relief expedition under Ivar Baadson, which came up the coast from the Eastern Settlement. It was formerly thought that the Western Settlers had been destroyed by the Eskimos. Archaeological research, published in *Meddelelser Om Gronland*, however, now hints that the settlers may have emigrated *en masse*, leaving some of their cattle at large behind them. Since they returned neither to the Eastern Settlement, nor to Iceland, nor anywhere else that we know of, it seems only reasonable to suppose that this final migration of Norse-Irish people went to America and somewhere there the traces of them should be sought.

Before we leave them, let us just try to picture these people, some of whose ancestors had in all probability come to Britain as long ago as the age of Megalith builders, others from Central Europe and others again from Norway, as they set out on their last expedition. Their ships were sewn together with baleen and their axe-heads were cut from whale-bones, for iron was now so scarce in Greenland. Their cooking pots and lamps were carved from soap-stone and their buckles were made from ivory instead of bronze. Their rough homespun clothes, however, were still cut in the fashions of far-off Europe and they were Christian men and women. Much had been lost, but nothing could really conquer the spirit of adventure in an indomitable people.

It would have made a great saga had anyone been able to

piece it altogether at the time. It has, however, remained for the historian and archaeologist to do so, little by little, from innumerable small and apparently trivial scraps of information. No civilized Romano-Briton of the third century, living in comfort on his farm in modern Gloucestershire, could possibly have dreamed that his remote descendants, using bone battle-axes, might end their days fighting Red Indians on the shores of an unknown continent.

What happened to the people left behind in the Eastern Settlement of Greenland? Unaccustomed as we are ever to find anything that we can really understand in early history, the story for once seems to be fairly clear almost up to the end.

At first the Greenland Settlers established a republic on the same lines as they had in Iceland. Iceland was converted to Christianity in about 1000 A.D., and, while Eric was still alive, a priest arrived at Brattahlid. To be sure, Eric did not like him much and spoke of him as 'that hypocrite', but he did nothing worse than that. Christianity spread rapidly. By the beginning of the twelfth century, the country felt the need for a resident bishop who could ordain priests and keep them in order. A bishop was an expense to a poor community, but the need was great.

The story of the way in which the bishop came to be appointed is told in the *Flatey-Book*. At that time Sokki Thorisson was living at Brattahlid, which was evidently regarded as the central point in the country. He sent his son, Einar, armed with bribes of walrus-teeth and hides to King Sigurd Jorsalfar (the Crusader) in Norway. Eventually Bishop Arnald was consecrated at Lund in Sweden and, after staying a winter in Iceland, he reached Greenland about 1127 A.D. Greenland would have seemed less strange to him, coming from Norway, than Zanzibar to an English bishop of today.

A cathedral was built at Gardar on the opposite side of the firth to Brattahlid. It is uncertain whether the site originally chosen was not in the Western Settlement near Godthaab. At any rate, Gardar became the centre of religious activity in

Greenland for some three hundred years. The church has been carefully excavated. The grave of one bishop has been found in it, with his remains accompanied by a beautifully carved walrus-ivory crozier and his gold episcopal ring. The crozier shows clearly that such things as the enamelled crozier heads made at Limoges in the Middle Ages were not unknown in Iceland or Norway. The bishop's palace, his cow byres, his hay and tithe barns, his smithy and his midden have all been excavated. The church itself, together with others in Greenland, is quite unlike the former wooden 'stave church' at Skallaholt in Iceland or those of Norway. Experts, such as Aage Roussell, believe that its construction was influenced by churches in Scotland. The Gardar church, however, and some of the others, although mostly built of stone, had a wooden west end. This was probably elaborately carved, possibly in the style of interlacing dragons still to be seen on the church of Urness in Norway.

The houses of Greenland were from the first much like those of Iceland; long turf walls lined with wooden panels, low roofs and a fire down the middle. Sometimes a spring of water was led through a stone-lined channel across the hall. This served the double purpose of providing water for household work and also as a protection if some ill-disposed persons attempted to burn the roof over the inmates' heads at night. As time went on, the increasing cold and the shortage of firewood led to a change from these long houses to what is called a passage house. Numerous small rooms all opening off a central alley-way present a plan not unlike that of some Romano-British villas in Britain. It is thought that this idea was evolved in Greenland and spread back to Iceland.

The Bishop of Greenland could keep perhaps forty small cows and many sheep alive over the winter. They had to be closely packed in long sheds and protected from the cold by thick turf walls. You can still see from the stone-lined stalls exactly how many cows were kept at Gardar. The cows were smaller than any others in the north.

Owing to the shortage of wood and peat, the smelting of iron, which was normally carried out at home on an Icelandic farm, presented great difficulties. At Gardar, animal bones had to be used for fuel in the smithy. The birch scrub was soon cut down and all the drift-wood collected off the beaches. Iron had to be imported when possible from abroad. This had to be paid for in exported goods. Greenland cloth became famous, but the most valuable export was walrus-ivory. Every summer expeditions were sent far north up the west coast to bring back walrus-teeth and hides. It is thought that the most usual hunting-ground was in the neighbourhood of Disko, and I have seen a storehouse built by the Norsemen near Nugssuag, just north of the Vaigat, a sound which separates Disko Island from the mainland much as the Sound of Mull does that island from Morven. In many ways the Vaigat might well be the Sound of Mull during the Ice Age, or the Kyles of Loch Alsh and Rhae.

The Norsemen, however, sometimes went much further north than this. In a cairn on an island near Upernivik, in latitude 72°55° N., was found a small stone inscribed with runes. Expert opinion has differed as to the date of this stone, which may perhaps be 1333 A.D. It is, however, clear that Erling Sigvatsson, Bjarni Thordarson and Einridi Oddson, put it there the Saturday before the 25th of April some time in the fourteenth century. They must have spent the winter there. Suggestions that some hunters may have gone much farther north, even beyond the Devil's Thumb and ice-filled Melville Bay, which was so much dreaded by the nineteenth-century whalers, are to be found in the excavations carried out by Holtved in 1937 at the place now known as Thule. In the Eskimo middens and houses in this district pieces of Norse homespun, bone playing-men and Norse combs were found, which presumably reached the Eskimos in trade for walrus-tusks. Since the later days of the Norse settlement are certainly bound up with the doings of the Eskimos, it is necessary to try and learn something about them.

When the early settlers came to Greenland, they are said to have found traces of Scraelings, as they called them, both in the Eastern and Western Settlements. No Eskimos themselves were apparently seen except on the Wineland expeditions. Mention of trolls on the east coast of Greenland by Norsemen returning from there suggests that Eskimos were living on that side of the country. Archaeologists, however, have not found the slightest trace of ancient Eskimo remains south of Disko. Some of the remains on Disko may date back before contact was made with the Norsemen. Somewhere about 1200 A.D., however, Norse hunters met some little men who 'lack iron entirely, use the teeth of walrus for throwing weapons and use sharp stones for knives'. The Norsemen appear to have killed some of them, for the account includes a description, as Nørlund pointed out, of how they bleed when they are dead after being struck with weapons.

Remains of early Eskimo settlements must surely have existed further south. The Norsemen may have removed the stones of their tent rings for other purposes, but it seems most unlikely that no trace will ever be found.

As I have said before, the Eskimo depends for his survival through the winter on hunting from the ice. If the ice, as it appears, was further to the north in the early years of the Norse settlement, then to the north the Eskimo would have retired. He might come south in the summer to hunt the caribou or reindeer, in which case nothing but the rings of stones, which held down the edges of his tupecks, or skin tents, would remain, with an occasional small burial cairn. Nothing would be preserved on these tent-ring sites, save perhaps the point of a stone knife, a stone ulo blade, or an arrow-head. The enormous mass of objects which we find further north preserved by the cold in the middens and winter houses would not be there.

This preservation of things by the cold is a lesson to archaeologists in Britain. From one winter house on an island in Melville Bay, we returned with several packing cases full of objects: wooden dolls, toy boats, tub staves, box bottoms, arrow shafts, and lamp trimmers; bone toggles, dolls, pins, harpoons, foreshafts, swivels, knife-handles, drill-pieces, scraper-handles and snow-knives; baleen boxes, amulets, fragments of mattresses and a host of other things. The

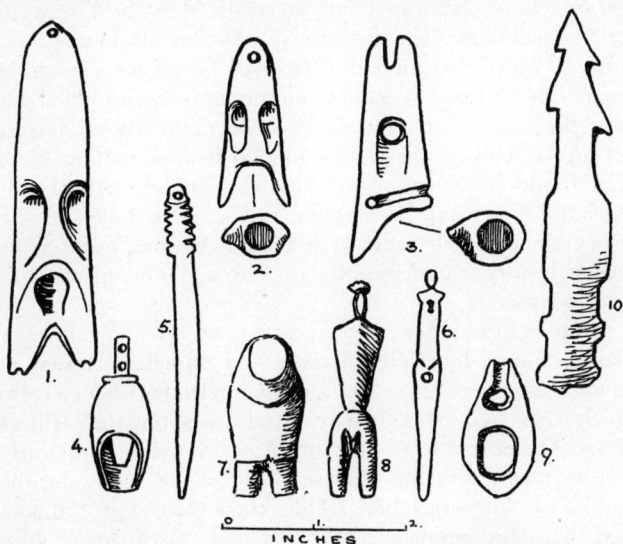

SOME TYPICAL ESKIMO OBJECTS OF ABOUT THE TIME OF THE END OF THE NORSE SETTLEMENTS

1—3. Ivory harpoons.   4. Ivory line-swivel.   5—6. Ivory bodkins
7. Wooden doll representing a Norseman.   8. Wooden doll representing an Eskimo woman with top-knot.   9. Bone dog-trace buckle.   10. Bone bird-dart barb.   [*From a hut site on Melville Bay, West Greenland.*

number of stone objects, however, was limited to one scraper blade. It is easy to see then, that where the process of natural decay is not arrested the only object to be preserved would be a single flint scraper. On an open tent-ring in southern Greenland nothing would have survived, but this one thing. Where in Britain you may find a couple of flint implements

and perhaps a scrap or two of pottery, a whole host of bone
and wooden implements would have mouldered in decay.

The origin of the Eskimos is still an unsolved problem.
Very much excellent work has been done by the Danes, but
still the real problem remains. Some people, like Sollas in his
Ancient Hunters, saw in them survivals from the European
Ice Age in France. There is probably some truth in this idea,
but it is much too limited. Traces of people in something
resembling an Eskimo stage of culture have been found near
Lake Baikal in Siberia and along its northern coast. Objects,
not unlike those of the earliest known Eskimo culture, have
been found in Norway and Sweden. Things perhaps not
unrelated to it have been found in the Swiss lakes, in the
Orkneys and the Hebrides. The Eskimo culture, as far as its
ancient history is understood, is not free from contacts with
other peoples.

As far as I can judge, the earliest known Eskimo culture of
Alaska, found by Helge Larsen and Froelich Rainey at
Ipiutak near the Behring Strait, contains elements drawn from
widely separated areas. It may date from about the birth of
Christ. The people who came into America with it had clearly
been in touch with the Chinese world to the south and the
peoples of Northern Siberia. They knew the use of iron, and
used it for the points of engraving tools to ornament their
harpoons and the ivory masks of their magicians. They carved
elaborate copies of iron chains and swivels out of ivory and
bone. They, however, fashioned the most delicate and
beautiful points for their arrows and blades for their knives
and harpoons out of flint. Their houses were in process of
adaptation from those of people living in temperate climes to
ones suitable for an arctic winter. We seem to be watching the
change from a people who had known a higher culture into
the conditions of Gordon-Childe's 'primitive communists' of
Skara Brae. The Eskimos may in fact be the remnants of what
was once an advanced and widespread culture in Europe and
Asia, who had been dispossessed and driven into America by

more warlike peoples. The present-day inhabitants of Tibet may easily be a branch of the same stock. The Ainu of Japan are possibly another. Elements may have been driven down into Indonesia. All this is yet in the stage of conjecture. Even when the Eskimos reached Greenland, I feel that they may have sometimes had contact with Western Europe, and traces of this may lie at the bottom of the Irish stories of Tir-nan-Og and the 'Land of Women'.

The earliest known Eskimo culture in Greenland is spoken of as the Cape Dorset. Its age is as yet uncertain, but it survived long enough for some of its objects to be found mixed with the succeeding culture, which the Danes have named as Thule. I do not like this name as it suggests connexions with Iceland, but so much has been published about it that it is probably too late to alter it. Larsen also speaks of the Thule Culture as the 'Arctic Whaling Culture', which is more descriptive and better in every way. These people were whalers and hunted from umiaks. The Cape Dorset people, whose relics have been mostly found in Arctic Canada, hunted with bows and speared fish and seals with harpoons. I have found their culture mixed with that of the Arctic whalers on North Devon Island and on Ellesmere Land north of Smith Sound. Holtved has found the same mixture on the opposite coast of Greenland.

The existence of the Cape Dorset people was first demonstrated by Diamond Jenness, who found the remains of their flint work in the south of Baffin Land near Hudson Strait. An enormous mass of their beautifully carved harpoons, bone needles and tiny representations of bears, birds, walrus and wolves, has since been collected by Graham Rowley at Iglulik in Northern Baffin Land. The only house sites, as far as I know, which may have belonged to them, and which have yet been excavated, are those I found in 1937 at Cape Hardy on North Devon Island.* The Cape Dorset people did not know

*'Archaeological Data from the Canadian Arctic', *Anthropological Journal*, 1939.

the use of the bow drill, and fashioned all their very delicate bone work with little curved stone knives, not unlike the Stone Age knives of Japan. The Cape Dorset people used

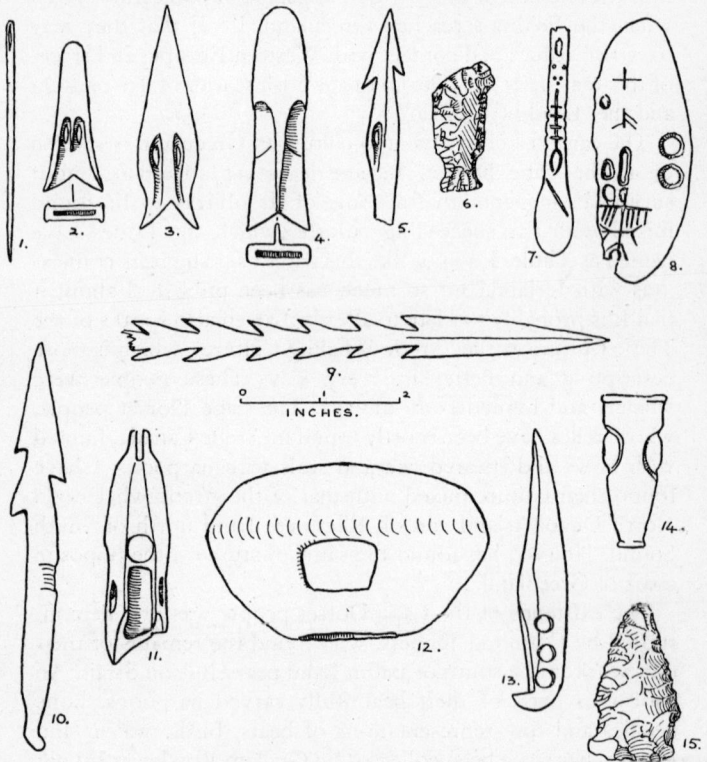

SOME TYPICAL ESKIMO OBJECTS COMPARED

1—9. Cape Dorset Culture. 10—15 Arctic Whaling Culture.

(1—5 *and* 9 *collected by G. Rowley. The remainder from my own excavations.*)
1. Bone needle. 2, 3, 4 and 11. Harpoons. 5 and 10. Bird dart barbs.
6 and 15. Flint knife points. 9 and 13. Laester barbs (?9). 7. Bone pendant. 8. Bone Box-bottom. 12. Ulo handle. 14. Bone Needle-case.

boat-shaped blubber-lamps of soap-stone. The later people used oval stone lamps, with a transverse ledge to hold the wicks of moss. The Scraelings of Wineland met by the early Norsemen may have been this people. Those who left before the Norsemen came to Greenland might have been the same.

Some Eskimo and American-Indian cultures appear to have remained almost unchanged for hundreds of years once they had been developed. The now extinct original Eskimos of Southampton Island remained in the Arctic Whaling Culture for perhaps two thousand years. The Cape Dorset people may have done the same. I think they would have had much in common with the men of the Oban caves and the Oransay Beaches, but they were apparently far more skilled with the stone knife.

Later Eskimo phases of culture in Greenland show unmistakable contacts with the Norse Settlers. They learnt the use of coopered wooden vessels. They modified the construction of their umiaks from an examination of the Norsemen's wooden boats. They made wooden dolls for their children in the forms of Norsemen. Although both peoples often killed one another, their contacts seem sometimes to have been peaceful. They exchanged homespun cloth for walrus-ivory no doubt, and very likely other things besides. Both peoples hunted seals and whales with harpoons. In the *Foster-Brothers Saga*, it says: 'When Thorgrim's ship came to land, people went down to the shore to see the finery of his arms and equipment and that of his crew. The Greenlanders always used to carry their hunting and fishing gear in their vessels. Thormod, who was also present, picked up a seal harpoon, which had been thrown ashore, and examined it'. In the Western Settlement the bones of the white-beaked dolphin, the ca'ing whale and the Right, or whalebone, whale have been identified by Dr. Degerbol in the Norse middens. Permission from the bishop had to be obtained before whales could be hunted in the fjords around Cape Farewell.

In the fourteenth century, when the climate became worse

and the ice came creeping down, the Eskimos followed it, and troubles increased. This same climatic change may have had some say in causing the English invasions of France and the Scottish raids into England. It is strange to think that the same conditions which sent English archers tramping to Crecy may also have sent Eskimos to shoot arrows at the Norse settlers in Greenland.

We have already seen how the worsening climate and the hostility of the Eskimos caused the Western Settlement to be abandoned by the middle of the fourteenth century. The Eastern Settlement, however, survived for many years. As late as 1408 A.D., a ship-load of Icelanders who had been blown off their course from Norway left Greenland for home. They were the last visitors of whom any record has survived. It is not probable, however, that they were the last.

For many years the trade with Greenland had been a close monopoly of the King of Norway and later, when that crown was joined to Denmark, in the hands of the Danish kings. A royal ship was supposed to sail once a year to Greenland and there were heavy punishments for anyone caught trading on his own account. The visits of the Royal Knorr, as the ship was called, became more and more infrequent. Some vessels were lost at sea. No bishops came out to take over the diocese: at last the ships ceased to come altogether. There are archaeological hints, however, that ships either from England or Germany, occasionally defied the royal ban. Scraps of pottery have been found which may take the story of the Eastern Settlement down to 1450 A.D. or so. This may perhaps explain the northern voyage of Cabot from Bristol. The memory of Greenland may have lingered on in Britain longer than is at present recognized.

The church and graveyard at Herjolfsness, near the Port of Sand, have been excavated. In the graveyard the clothes in which the remains of the last of the settlers were buried have been remarkably preserved. Liripipe hoods, long stockings and complete dresses of men, women and children were preserved by centuries of frost. They are of rather coarse homespun. By comparison with illustrations in books, it appears that the fashions of Western Europe were copied in Greenland down to about 1450 A.D. or even later. No other such wonderful collection of the everyday garments of an ancient farming population has been preserved anywhere in the world. The remarkable thing is that they followed the customs of dress in Western Europe in every detail. The Norse Settlers were still Europeans. They were not half-breed Eskimos dressed in skins, and at this point the story ends.

DRESS OF THE
NORSE SETTLERS IN
GREENLAND
AT THE BEGINNING OF
THE 15TH CENTURY A.D.

Both men and women wore long dresses of homespun with many pleats. Liripipe hoods and long stockings were worn by the men. The shoes are conjectured from those recently worn in Iceland. Otherwise the garments are based on actual specimens recovered from graves at Herjolfsness in Greenland and now preserved at Copenhagen. The man carries an axe made from whale's bone.

The skeletons at Herjolfsness were very badly preserved. At one time it was thought that they showed every sign of malnutrition, and that the women could not have borne children. This view is now disputed.

What happened to them? Were they all killed off, perhaps burnt in their churches as Eskimo legends suggest? Or did they too migrate? Are some of their descendants living today in the west country of England? Did they try their luck in America? If they came to England, nobody might have put it down in writing, for the ship which brought them would have been breaking the law. It would not surprise me if someone delving in the old archives of Bristol one day came upon a hint of this.

The end of the Eastern Settlement then, like that of the Western one, is quite unknown. Some day a farm may be excavated which shows clearly that it was destroyed by Eskimos. Long ago, Norse skulls are said to have been found with flint arrow-heads sticking in them, but they cannot now be traced. The Eskimos, when Hans Egede converted them to Christianity in the eighteenth century, told him tales of slaughtered Norsemen. There is, however, no archaeological trace of it whatever. One farm in the Western Settlement was found to have been deserted in a hurry. In about 1450 A.D. there were numerous Norsemen at Herjolfsness. About fifty years later an Icelander, nicknamed Jon Greenlander, said that he had found sheds, booths and stone houses for drying fish as in Iceland on a small island off the coast of Greenland. There was a dead man lying on the ground, wearing a well-made hood and clothes of frieze cloth and sealskin; by his side was a worn sheath-knife. This story may be quite true, but it tells us nothing. When John Davies visited the Western Settlement in 1585 and 1586 A.D., he found no living person, which is not strange, for Ivar Baadson had found none more than two hundred years before. We have not really the slightest idea what became of the people of the Eastern Settlement. I think, however, that they too departed by sea. Had they been overwhelmed, some trace would have remained. Life was becoming terribly uncomfortable at Herjolfsness. Food was getting scarce; iron was almost unobtainable; nobody came to buy their ivory and cloth. The Eskimos were a perpetual nuisance. Why not go and try again somewhere else?

I do not think it is necessary to go into Zeno's story of Sir Henry Sinclair, Earl of Orkney, who is said to have sailed to the West in about 1390 A.D. and found people with books which they could not read. Some say that the tale is altogether fictitious. I doubt this, for there was no point in an Italian nobleman making up lies about his ancestors and people he did not know. The tale, however, is so confused that Sinclair may only have sailed to Iceland and Greenland. He certainly appears to have reached both these countries. The description of a Greenland kayak is unmistakable. There remains however a strong possibility that he did go to America and that its existence was not unknown in Scotland at that time.

One curious incident remains to be discussed. Fifty years ago a dressed stone slab, now known as the Kensington Stone, was found by a Swedish settler in Minnesota, right in the middle of North America: carved on it was a long inscription in runes. The stone has long been the subject of controversy. Most scholars held the thing to be a fake. The inscription apparently reads: 'Eight Goths and twenty-two Norwegians on exploration journey from Vinland through the west. We camped by two skerries one day from this stone. We were fishing one day. When we came home we found ten men red with blood and dead. A.V.M. Save from evil. Have ten of our party by the sea to guard our ship fourteen days from this island. Year 1362.' The inscription of A.V.M. (*Ave Maria*) was in Roman lettering.

When it was found in 1898 A.D., the stone was said to have been under the roots of a tree many years old. The whole thing may, however, have been a carefully planted fake. If this is so, who did it? It is perfectly easy for unscrupulous people to make fakes and plant them. In this case, however, it could not have been done by anyone except a scholar with a wide knowledge of the subject. The runes are not those you would find in an ordinary text book, but the correct late runes of the period to which they are supposed to have belonged. Whoever had this fake made and planted, must also have had access to a document which was found apparently only in 1928 in the Royal Library at Copenhagen. This is an order dated 1354 A.D. to a certain Paul Knutson to take a Royal Knorr with a picked band of adventurers and go to Greenland to see whether the

colonists there were still observing the Christian religion. It
was signed on behalf of King Magnus Erikson by Orm
Ostenson, the regent.

Those who believe the Kensington Stone to be genuine
think that Paul Knutson went on from Greenland to do
missionary work in America. If he did so, he must have passed
by way of Hudson Bay and ultimately up the Red River to
near its source. Was he, in fact, looking for the missing
settlers from the Godthaab district of Greenland?

The authenticity or otherwise of the Kensington Stone has
yet to be proved. It is, however, very hard to see who could
have had the knowledge to make such a fake. Almost any
scholar in the world who wished to prove the former existence
of Norsemen in America, would have had the stone carved in
eleventh-century runes and dumped on the shore near whatever place on the east coast of America be believed to have
been Wineland. The number of people who could possibly
have known of King Magnus' fourteenth-century order to
Knutson years before it was published must almost be so
limited as to rule the possibility of faking out of court. The
betting is hundreds to one against it being a fake. The stone is
said to be native to the place where it was found. There is no
real reason to suppose that the finder was not telling the truth.
If he was telling the truth, a tree had been growing above the
stone since about 1850 A.D., at which time the country round
about was still unpeopled except by Indians and hunters. If the
stone is a fake, it must have been the work of a demented scholar
of great learning. It is a regular 'Who done it?' The sceptics
must find the criminal before common-sense will accept their
case. If the stone is genuine, Wineland may not have been on
the east coast of America at all, but have been reached by way
of Hudson Bay. This is a problem for Americans to tackle.

CHAPTER NINE

THE CROFTING CULTURE

I HAVE NOW CARRIED the story right through the ages down to its climax, when the Greenland settlers disappear from human ken. In all its later stages it is the story of communities in one type of culture. They were crofters: that is to say, farmers who combined a little cultivation, a fair amount of fishing and a little hunting with a great deal of raising of sheep and cattle.

As far as I can see, this crofting culture probably resulted from the combination of the activities of the three earliest peoples we know in Scotland. The fishing came from the boatmen of Oban and Oransay; the stock-raising from the Beaker men; the Megalithic people grew a little corn. All three naturally engaged in hunting. The same process probably took place all over the north-western seaboard of Europe. All subsequent arrivals in Britain down to the Belgic Conquest were more or less in the same stage of culture. The Belgic and Roman conquerors had their ideas of agriculture developed to a much higher level. The Saxons, in the days of Cæsar, had not apparently reached the grain-cultivating stage at all, but by the time they came to Britain they had learnt to grow corn. Corn had been grown in Denmark at a very early period. Plough teams, wagons and light carts or war chariots are shown on the Scandinavian rock-engravings of the Bronze Age. Actual wooden ploughs have been found. The Norsemen who came to Britain were certainly in the crofting stage. It lasted on in Iceland more or less to the present day and is still in full swing in the Hebrides. The true crofter community, however, should include sea-fishing among its occupations. This to some extent is being lost owing to the activities of the big trawlers. The old crofter's fishing was mostly done with hook and line; now, where he can still afford a boat, he often uses the herring net.

The combination of fishing with stock-raising was most important for the health of the people. This was especially true in northern latitudes, where few cattle could be kept alive over the winter. The mixed diet of milk and fish products kept the people in good health. The Icelandic cod-fishing took place in the winter. It was very dangerous; even in saga times we hear of boats being lost.

At the beginning of the Norse settlement in Iceland we are told of men cultivating fields of grain. This would certainly have been dried artificially as it was in some parts of Roman Britain. The *King's Mirror*, a document of the early thirteenth century, states that some rich men in Greenland attempted it as an experiment. With the deterioration of climate, corn-growing almost, if not quite, died out even in Iceland; in Greenland it was hopeless.

From the earliest times corn has had to be ground before it can be made into bread. This was carried out for many ages by rubbing one stone on top of another. About fifty years before the birth of Christ, a form of quern was introduced, which consisted of two circular stones, one fitting on a pivot on top of the other. The top stone was rotated by hand and it was very hard work for the women. The Romans brought a small 'undershot' form of water-mill into Britain. Remains of mill-wheels and iron spindles have been found. It is said that the water-mill was introduced into Ireland from Scotland (Alba) about 230 A.D., because the high king, Cormac, did not like to see his concubine, Ciarnait, a Pictish princess, working so hard at a hand quern. This may very well be approximately correct. Whether the Norse used a water-mill before they settled in Scotland is unknown to me. They made use of such mills in later times. The ruins of quite a number may be seen here and there in the west of Scotland. Some complete buildings survive in the Faeroes; I have not noticed one in Iceland.

One of the most elusive peoples of antiquity is the Pictish race, or Cruithnigh. Whatever their origin may have been, whether at first they were only a small ruling caste or the whole Celtic people of Britain, it is clear that their later rulers were matrilineal. A king of the Hebrides, for instance, was allowed to own no wife or property, but could help himself to those of his subjects. It is usually thought that they were a people who tattooed themselves. If this is so, it is most interesting to observe that the witches of later years also tattooed themselves. The witches clearly practised some form of nature-worship and had a fertility cult. One of the districts where persecutions for witchcraft were most numerous after the Middle Ages was eastern Scotland, north of the Forth, where Chadwick believes the Pictish people, who built the Gallic Wall forts, first established themselves. Other districts where witchcraft was rife were the west of England outside the limits of the Belgic Conquest and the Icenian territory of East Anglia. It seems possible that the witches were carrying on a religion which was prevalent in Britain in pre-Belgic times. This religion was probably spread all over north-western Europe, and dates back to the earliest herdsmen, if not before. Whether the Druids were what would now be called witches, I cannot say, but I should think it is most improbable. The highlander believes that the rowan tree will keep witches away, and the rowan was venerated by the Irish Druids. If these conclusions are right, there were at least two strata of religious belief in Scotland before the coming of Christianity. Analytical treatment of the mass of folklore which has been collected in the Highlands might be able to separate the two creeds. There were clearly two different systems of reckoning descent. The Picts were matrilineal according to Bede and others, and the Scots patrilineal. There were also apparently two religions, druidism and witchcraft. As well as this, there was a form of Welsh language and also Gaelic. There may well be some way of separating these facts into two groups and applying the one to the people of the brochs and the other to the men of the Gallic Walls. If, however, one attempts this, one finds that both druidism and witchcraft belong to the Gallic Wall districts and we are no farther forward. Witchcraft is probably much older than druidism.

From a material point of view, there is practically no difference between the cultures which are now slowly dying out in Wales, Ireland, Western Scotland, the Faeroes, Norway and Iceland. The culture of the Norse settlers in Greenland was the same. There can be no doubt that any useful idea passed easily in any direction by sea. It probably travelled with greater speed than it did by land. No one people can claim to have originated the culture. It was the combined output of the minds of many men in many lands but had nothing in common with the ideas of the Roman Empire or Feudal Europe. A few simple devices might be borrowed, like the crusie and the water-mill, but in the main it was quite independent.

It is clear, I think, that the Norsemen were by no means the first visitors to Iceland. Even if the accounts of Pytheas are doubted, Ptolemy shows a large island named Thule well to the north of Scotland, which can hardly be a confusion with the Shetlands or Faeroes. The Irish monks are known to have been going to Iceland for centuries before the Norsemen.

The question of Greenland is not so easy. I have already discussed the matter to some extent in a former book. It is still a matter of guessing at probabilities. We have ancient Irish stories of long sea-voyages to far-off lands beyond the sunset. Some scholars believe these to be symbolic of visits to a future world. This seems improbable to me and I think they are myths and contain vague traditions of actual voyages. A case, too, can be made out for some connexion in material things between the men of the Eskimo Arctic Whaling Culture and the people of Britain during the Roman period. This case rests on very slender foundations. It is no more than a hint. There is the curious resemblance, too, between the whale-flensing blubber-mattocks of the Scottish Iron Age and those of the Eskimo whalers. The Scottish examples probably belong to the Roman period. Nobody has as yet identified an Eskimo culture of this date in Greenland. I have, however, given reasons to show why this might happen, even if Eskimos had been there at that time. The case for visits to Greenland by seamen coming from the Roman world is therefore so vague as to be little more than a possibility.

It is rather different when the voyages of the Irish monks are considered. There is no doubt in my mind that they made a very thorough investigation of the coast of Iceland and that fairly exact reports of their explorations were preserved at Iona, or in some similar centre, when the Norsemen began to settle in the Hebrides. I cannot explain the story of Orlyg in any other way without bringing in the supernatural. The story of Cormac shows that on occasions these monks could be blown over to the Greenland coasts. I find it very hard to believe that, having explored the coasts and learnt the possibilities of Iceland, some monks did not carry the matter a stage further and visit Greenland. As far as one can judge, there would be no ice to hinder their passage round Cape Farewell. I think it most probable that some anchorites may have used islands off the south west coast of Greenland for their meditations. They could have done this without using Iceland as a stopping-place on the way. Cape Farewell is on practically the same parallel of latitude as Cape Wrath. In the last years of sailing ships, the English West-Country fish schooners used to set a course for Newfoundland which took them right up to the edge of the ice off Cape Farewell. They were known to make the whole transatlantic passage in a fortnight, or three weeks at the most. Three men and a boy made up the crew. This kind of thing is easily forgotten. The North Atlantic seems an enormous area, but if a curragh could make the passage to Iceland it could do the same to Greenland.

The possibility of finding ancient habitations of Celtic anchorites on the Greenland islands must be borne in mind. Care too must be taken to distinguish them from Eskimo ruins.

I will leave this study with the picture of a great, grey, waste of tumbled seas. One tiny black dot is skimming over its surface. Day after day this dot flies northward. No friendly plume of smoke trails across the sky. Nothing is seen but the fulmars and shearwaters incessantly gliding over the wave tops, the tiny stormy petrels paddling on the water, or the occasional blow of a whale. Bearded, dirty, salt-caked men sit gazing out at the ever changing ocean. At night strange lights flicker in the sky, like a car's headlights seen over the top of a hill. Then one day the scream of terns is heard and soon high, jagged, blue mountains streaked with white, appear on the horizon. The 'desert' has been reached.

NOTES

1. PALÆOLITHIC MAN IN SCOTLAND (*page* 5)

Although Palæolithic man was apparently well-established in Yorkshire, archaeologists have not found it easy to find signs of him in Scotland. There seems to be no real reason why he should not have lived there.

At Inchnadamph in Sutherland, a limestone cave, at a considerable height above sea level, was found to contain the remains of numerous reindeer killed for food. As, however, these do not appear to have been accompanied by any characteristic implements of Palæolithic man and, as it is stated in the *Orkneyinga Saga* that the Norsemen hunted reindeer in Northern Scotland, the Inchnadamph remains may belong to almost any period we like to suggest.

2. RAISED BEACHES (*page* 6)

The whole question of raised beaches is extremely difficult. Clearly a raised beach may be formed in at least two different ways: it may be produced by a raising of the level of the land, or by a lowering of the level of the sea.

It is clear that before an area can be covered by a great ice sheet much water must be removed from the sea by evaporation and then deposited upon the land in the form of snow. When huge areas of the world were covered by sheets of ice thousands of feet in thickness, the sea level must have been lowered to an appreciable extent. Raised beaches would then appear on every shore in the world. There must therefore have been raised beaches corresponding to each major glaciation. With the melting of the ice, these beaches should have returned to normal sea-level. Raised beaches, however, are still found all over the world at considerable heights above the modern sea-level, and it is doubtful if there is still enough water locked up in the ice fields of Greenland and Antarctica to account for them.

The beaches, formed by the lowering of the surface of the land and its subsequent emergence, are less difficult to follow. I have little doubt that they were frequently caused by the enormous weight of the ice sheets, which depressed the crust of the earth beneath them. The process of re-emergence, however, seems to have been most uneven. In Western Scotland there appear to be at least two post-glacial raised beaches. In the north of Baffin Bay, on the Cary Islands, I have observed a series of raised beaches rising in terraces for several hundreds of feet. These terraces, which differ in level by only a few feet at a time, may be thought to represent a gradual contraction of the Polar Ice Cap. This, however, was clearly not a steady process, for in North Devon Island and in Melville Bay ancient Eskimo houses can be seen below the level of the highest tides of today. In other words, if the theory of depression by the weight of the ice sheet is correct, the level of some areas in the north has been depressed since the days of the Norse Settlements in Greenland. This is probably correct, but it does not account for the sinking of large areas in the west of Scotland in historic times. It is true that there was till recently a small ice carapace on Ben Nevis, but there is no suggestion that much of Scotland was covered by ice in the sixteenth century or so.

It seems to me that the depression of the land by an ice sheet followed by emergence when the ice melts must set in process a wave, or see-saw, movement which gradually diminishes in intensity. The land probably springs up above its normal level when the weight is released and slowly goes up and down till equilibrium is attained. If this is correct, beach levels will not be datable in direct, but in alternate, sequences. Not only is this the case, but allowance must also be made for the rising and lowering of sea levels by water taken up and released by ice sheets. There is no simple solution to the raised beach problem.

3. DATING OF EARLY PERIODS (*page* 10)

The absolute dating of times for which no written evidence exists is of course impossible. The dating of early rulers and events in Egypt can, however, be described as something approximating to history. A date in the eighteenth Dynasty in Egypt has been checked astronomically by the mention of the helical rising of Sirius, and the duration of the eighteenth Dynasty has been dated with some accuracy between 1587 and 1375 B.C. After this Egyptian dating is probably fairly accurate. Before this period, the authorities, Petrie and Breasted, differed in their estimates by a considerable number of years. Petrie estimated the Proto-Dynastic period of Egypt to have lasted from about 4777 to 4998 B.C., while Breasted suggested a duration from about 3400 to 2900 B.C. When such a wide difference may be observed in the views of scholars dealing with a semi-historical period, it is clear that very great caution must be used in accepting the assurances of scholars as to the dating of events in Britain, whose people kept no written records.

Walther Bremer, the late keeper of Antiquities in the National Museum of Ireland, in a posthumous essay entitled *Ireland's Place in Prehistoric and Early Historic Europe*, remarked: 'This climactic period of Ireland is the First Period of the Bronze Age, which is to be dated about 2500-1900 B.C. . . . . . I cannot enter into reasons which induce me to maintain this longer dating, against the efforts of Childe (*Archaeologia*, IXXIV, 1925, p. 159 ff.), and especially of Reinecke (*Götze-Festschrift*, 1925), to maintain the probability of a shorter dating. So complex are the relations between the whole series of cultures and culture-areas in Central Europe during the Neolithic and Bronze Ages, that to me the only possible way to obtain an absolute chronology in Northern Europe seems to be that which Hubert Schmidt has deduced from the Ægean, over Spain and Ireland (see *Prähistorische Zeitschrift*, 1 (1909), p. 124 ff.) Here we find the equations: Early Minoan I=Bell-Beakers: Early Minoan III=Troy II=Monteracello= El Argar=Ireland Bronze Age I.'

I have no idea which of these two groups of pundits may be right, and leave it to the reader's common-sense to decide how much faith to put in the dates we see happily quoted in textbooks.

One reliable time scale appears to exist. This is a computation based on the layers of deposit left by the last great ice sheet on its yearly retreat. De Geer counted these layers from Denmark northwards over Sweden. From his counts it appears that the ice left the northern parts of Sweden about eight thousand years ago.

Perhaps the most hopeful method of establishing an accurate chronology is still in its infancy. This consists of comparing the yearly rings of growth in pieces of ancient wood found on sites with objects of recognizable cultures. It is already possible to recognize a general conformity of the relative thicknesses of these rings over wide areas of southern Britain. Most of the Roman period has now been covered and in time this will be extended so that a chart of yearly variations can be recognized extending back at least to the earliest Bronze Age peat growths. When this has been done, it will be possible to count the number of years between the Roman and perhaps the Neolithic periods. As far as one can judge, this method could be very reliable and would completely supersede the estimates of the present day.

4. SOME PROBLEMATIC PEOPLES OF SCOTLAND (*page* 50)

While I do not feel competent to make any attempt at guessing the origin of such peoples as the Tuath de Danan, the Fir Bolg, or the Milesians, there remain two rather mysterious peoples about whom something might be said.

The Attacotti

These people are mentioned for the first time in Roman sources in the fourth century A.D., and later appear as supplying units to the Roman army. They have been described as cannibals and as complete savages. Various scholars have identified them with the Aitheach Tuath, and some have suggested that they represented the older portions of the Irish people, subject to the later Celtic immigrants. This may be the case; but it should be remembered that 'Aith', or some closely similar word, was the Irish equivalent of the Highland 'Sith' (or Shee). They were elves, goblins or something of the kind. Traditionally they were the people who shot flint-tipped arrows at you as you walked along a lonely road.

It seems to me that 'Aitheach' in the fourth century may

have been a term adopted as a military designation by Celtic troops serving in the Roman Army; in the same way as other units adopted terms like 'tonnantes'. The Attacotti who attacked Britain may then have been time-expired soldiery trained in the Roman army and calling themselves 'the Demons' to express their ferocity.

The Lochlannach

Most scholars believe that the men of Lochloinn were Norwegians. It is even thought that the name refers to a definite part of western Norway. Ridgeway, on the other hand, believed them to have come from Scotland; from the Longos or Longus of Ptolemy, which appears to be the modern Lorne .The Lochlannach, although the name seems to be the Gaelic equivalent of 'Vikings', are mentioned in Irish writings as early as the second century A.D. Una, mother of Conn of the hundred battles, was the daughter of the King of Lochloinn. Men of Lochloinn even appear to have invaded Ulster in the first century B.C.

In *The Dream of Rhonabwy* (*Mabinogion*) the men of Llychlyn, under March (Marcus), came to help Arthur at the battle of Badon against the Saxons under Osla big-knife.

Now, while the later use of Lochlannach may well refer to Vikings settled in western Scotland, it is hard to see how the term could be applied in the earlier period. Its change of use may well be equivalent to that of 'gall', which in later times meant a foreigner, but must surely in earlier ones have referred to a 'Gaul' or Welshman.

I think it may be possible to approach the problem from a different angle. Scattered about the Hebrides are numerous stone forts, many of which bear the same name 'Dun nighean righ Lochlainn' (The fort of the daughter of the King of Lochloinn). That not one of these forts is of Viking origin is almost a certainty, but then very few of the Iron Age hill forts named after Oliver Cromwell were built by him! On the other hand, this naming of forts after the daughter of a king is a remarkable thing. Why not call them after the King himself? The answer surely is that these forts did not belong to the Kings. They were the property of the women, and the King only became King when he married the daughter of the previous Queen. In other words, the Lochlannach were matrilineal like the Picts. Not one of these forts is a broch. The best preserved specimen I have seen, in Loch Uskavagh in Benbecula, a fort which has somehow escaped the report of the Royal Commission on Ancient Monuments, may prove on examination to be of murus-gallicus construction.

The picture begins to take shape. Ptolemy places the 'Creones' in the general area of the great lochs. 'Creones' appears to be an attempt at the name 'Cruithnigh'. The Cruithnigh were Picts, a Welsh-speaking race of Gauls. The Picts were matrilineal. The Lochlannach appear to have been matrilineal also. It looks to me as if Ridgeway were perfectly correct in the view that the Lochlannach came from Scotland. It seems, that the original Lochlannach were probably a branch of the Gallic Wall people settled round the of Firth of Lorne or Loch Loinn.

A hint that both broch and Gallic Wall peoples were of Gaulish origin may perhaps be found in the name Dun nan Gall, which is attached to some brochs.

5. DRESS OF THE CELTS (*page* 60)

It is usually assumed that the original dress of the Celts in Scotland and Ireland was the same as that known to have been worn by them in medieval times. This consisted of a linen tunic, or leinne, covered by a cloak or plaid. This, however, was certainly not the dress of the Celts when they were engaged in war with the Romans on the continent, or that of the Celts in Ireland at the time of the Cuchlainn Saga, which is thought to date before 150 A.D. at the latest. Down to this date, the dress of the Celts apparently consisted of a short tunic, breeches and a cloak. All this is fully described in Ridgeway's *Early Age of Greece*. At the time of Giraldus Cambrensis, in the twelfth century A.D., some Irishmen were still wearing breeches and shoes. In the fourteenth century, however, Froissart only mentions tunics and no breeches.

A warning, however, is necessary. Although we are told that the tribes outside the Belgic Area of Britain wore little or no dress at all in the early years of the Christian era, it is probable that they were often completely clothed. We have no idea what they wore, but textiles were certainly woven for hundreds of years before the Roman Conquest. It is by no means certain that the weave now known as 'tartan' was not used in this country at a very early date. It was apparently known in Denmark in the Bronze Age. The tartan therefore does not appear to have been characteristic of any one people. Fragments of 'tartan' weaving appear in Saxon graves.

6. THE NORSE NAME FOR ARDNAMURCHAN (*page* 99)

The earliest notices of this most important geographical feature, which divides the Western Islands of Scotland into two groups, are to be found in Adamnan's life of St. Columba, which was written about 690 A.D. Here the name of the peninsula appears to have been Artda Muirchol. The translation of this name has presented great difficulties. W. J. Watson, in his *Celtic Place Names of Scotland*, seems to think that it could be translated as 'The Capes of Sea Wickedness' and its modern variant Ard na Murchen as 'the point of sea-hounds (otters)'.

There is, however, a hint that this name for the cape may not have been employed by the Norsemen. Just inside the mouth of the Sound is the extensive crofting township of Ormsaig. This name must surely have been derived from the Norse Orm's, or Serpent's, Bay. I have always assumed that Orm was a personal name indicating that a Viking named Ormr had settled there; but, on seeing the peninsula again recently, I feel that it is most probable that it was known to the Norsemen as the Serpent and is comparable to the Worm's Head and Great Orme's Head in southern Britain.

SHORT BIBLIOGRAPHY

GENERAL

BIRKET-SMITH, K.	*The Eskimos*	Methuen, 1936
BURY, J. B.	*The Invasion of Europe by the Barbarians*	Macmillan, 1928
BROOKS, C. E. P.	*Climate Through the Ages*	
CHILDE, V. G.	*Prehistoric Communities of the British Isles*	Chambers, 1940
COLLINGWOOD, R. G.	*Archaeology of Roman Britain*	Methuen, 1930
COON, C. S.	*The Races of Europe*	Macmillan, 1939
DANIEL, G. E.	*The Three Ages*	Cambridge, 1943
DECHELETTE, J.	*Manuel d'Archèologie*	Paris, 1914
FALCONER, W. and HAMILTON, H. C.	*Strabo's Geography*	Bohn's Libraries
FOORD, E.	*The Last Age of Roman Britain*	Harrap, 1925
GILES, J. A.	*Bede's Ecclesiastical History with the Anglo-Saxon Chronicle*	Bohn's Libraries
HODGKIN, R. H.	*A History of the Anglo-Saxons*	Oxford, 1935
HORNELL, J.	*British Coracles and Irish Curraghs*	Quaritch, 1938
	Water Transport	Cambridge, 1946
KENDRICK, T. D.	*A History of the Vikings*	Methuen, 1930
	The Druids	Methuen, 1927
RICHMOND, I.	*Roman Britain*	Collins, 1947
RIDGEWAY, SIR W.	*Early Age of Greece*	Cambridge, 1931

SHETELIG, H.   *Viking Antiquities in*
                     Great Britain & Ireland Oslo, 1940
(*With*Falk & Gordon)*Scandinavian Archaeology* Oxford, 1937
SOLLAS, W. J.   *Ancient Hunters*   Macmillan, 1924
THOMPSON, J. O.   *History of Ancient*
                     Geography   Cambridge, 1948
WILLIAMSON, K.   *The Atlantic Islands*   Collins, 1948
WRIGHT, W. B.   *The Quaternary Ice Age* London, 1937

SCOTLAND

ALLEN, J. ROMILLY   *Early Christian Monu-*
                     ments of Scotland   Edinburgh, 1903
Reports of the Royal Commission on Ancient and Historical
                     Monuments of Scotland

ANDERSON, A. O.   *Early Sources of*
                     Scottish History   1922

ANDERSON, J.   *Scotland in Pagan Times*
                     Scotland in Early
                     Christian Times   Edinburgh, 1883
                                              et seq.

BEVERIDGE, E.   *Coll and Tiree*
                     North Uist   Edinburgh, 1903

BREMNER, R. L.   *The Norsemen in Alban* Maclehose, Jack-
                                              son & Co., 1923

BROGGER, A. D.   *Ancient Emigrants*   Oxford, 1929

CHADWICK, H. M.   *Early Scotland*   Cambridge, 1949

CHILDE, V. G.   *Prehistory of Scotland* London, 1935
                     Scotland Before the Scots Methuen, 1946

CRAWFORD, O. G. S.   *The Topography of Roman*
                     Scotland   Cambridge, 1949

MACDONALD, SIR G.   *The Roman Wall in*
                     Scotland   Oxford, 1934

REEVES, W.   *Adamnan's Life of St.*
                     Columba   Dublin, 1857

SCOTT, SIR W. L.	*Problem of the Brochs* *Gallo-British Colonies*	Proceedings of the Prehistoric Society, 1947 and 1948
SKENE, W. F.	*Celtic Scotland*	Edmonston and Douglas, 1876
WATSON, W. J.	*History of the Celtic Place Names of Scotland*	Blackwood, 1926

ICELAND, Etc.

DASENT, G. W.	*The Story of Burnt Nial* *The Orkneyinga Saga*	Edmonston and Douglas, 1861
ELDJARN, K.	*Gengith a Reka*	Akureyri, 1948
ELLWOOD, T.	*The Book of the Settlement of Iceland*	Kendal, 1908
HERMANNSON, H.	*The Problem of Wineland*	Cornell University, 1936
JONASSEN, J.	*Islenzkir Thjòthaettir*	Reykjavik, 1934
MUNN, W. A.	*Wineland Voyages*	St. John's, Newfoundland, 1946
NØRLUND, P.	*Viking Settlers in Greenland*	Cambridge, 1936
SWANTON, J. R.	*The Wineland Voyages*	Smithsonian Institute, 1947